# BOATING 101

## Essential Lessons for Boaters

# ROGER H. SIMINOFF

INTERNATIONAL MARINE/McGRAW-HILL

CAMDEN, MAINE · NEW YORK · SAN FRANCISCO · WASHINGTON, D.C. ·
AUCKLAND · BOGOTÁ · CARACAS · LISBON · LONDON · MADRID ·
MEXICO CITY · MILAN · MONTREAL · NEW DELHI · SAN JUAN ·
SINGAPORE · SYDNEY · TOKYO · TORONTO

# International Marine

*A Division of The **McGraw-Hill** Companies*

10 9 8 7 6 5 4 3 2

Library of Congress Cataloging-in-Publication Data
Siminoff, Roger H.
      Boating 101 : essential lessons for boaters / by Roger H. Siminoff
         p.       cm.
    ISBN 0-07-134329-6 (alk.paper)
      1. Boats and boating—Safety measures. 2. Seamanship. I. Title.
  II. Title: Boating one hundred one.
  GV777.55.S53 1999
  797.1'028'9—dc21                         98-53518
                                              CIP

Questions regarding the content of this book should be addressed to:
International Marine
P.O. Box 220
Camden, ME 04843
Visit us on the World Wide Web at www.internationalmarine.com

Questions regarding the ordering of this book should be addressed to:
The McGraw-Hill Companies Customer Service Department
P.O. Box 547
Blacklick, OH 43004
Retail customers: 1-800-262-4729 Bookstores: 1-800-722-4726

This book is printed on 70# Citation, an acid-free paper.

Printed by R. R. Donnelley, Crawfordsville, IN
Design by Carol Inouye, Inkstone Communications Design
Production management by Janet Robbins
Page layout by Deborah Evans
Production Assistance by Shannon Thomas
Illustrations by Rob Groves
Boat icon by Carol Inouye
Edited by Jonathan Eaton and John Vigor
All photographs by the author

# DEDICATION

To my mother, Ruth,
for breathing the wind into my sails
and teaching me to always look beyond the horizon

# CONTENTS

## Tip 1.5 Respect the lifelines and stay inside them

Most boats have *lifelines* around their perimeter. The supporting framework usually is made up of metal stanchions (vertical posts) secured to the deck at 5- or 6-foot intervals, with a metal "pulpit," (a narrow balustrade-like structure) at the bow and a similar "pushpit" at the stern. The lifelines (lightweight cables) are strung between these fixtures.

The term "lifelines" shouldn't be taken too literally. The fixtures that typically make up this perimeter fence are seldom rugged enough to guarantee that a 150-pound person, tossed against the lines with moderate force, will be kept from going overboard. For your safety, and the safety of everyone aboard, remember these tips:

The entire crew should always be well within the perimeter of the boat, never seated on the lifelines or railings.

1. Don't allow your crew or passengers to sit on a lifeline. The lines or shackles *can* break, and someone could get dumped overboard by the jolt of, for example, suddenly hitting the wake of another vessel.

2. Don't allow your crew or passengers to secure their heavy-weather harnesses to a lifeline. Instead, secure them to something inboard such that at full extension of the harness, the crewmember ends up *at* a lifeline but not beyond it (see Tip 9.4).

3. Assure that lifeline shackles, or "pelican hooks," are securely fastened *before* you leave the dock. (When I'm racing or cruising for a period of time, I tape the shackles closed to ensure they won't open unexpectedly.)

## Tip 1.6  The best places to tie fenders

Many skippers are in the habit of tying fenders to the lifelines. After all, it's easier than bending down to tie them to the base of the stanchion. Additionally, some companies make clips that help you clip your fenders onto the lifelines without tying them each time.

There are several things to consider here: First, when you're alongside a dock or rafting up with another vessel (see Tip 5.22), surge can cause an up-and-down or rocking movement along the line of contact. That movement can generate great force against the fender and, subsequently, against the lifelines. Lifelines are strong but when subjected to great loads, the lines and fittings can be stretched or broken. Also, the leverage imposed by exerting force at the top lifeline can bend or break the stanchions.

Some skippers will even tie fenders to their cabintop grabrails. While this is a better solution than tying to the lifelines, I have also seen grabrails break when a heavy surge and the subsequent mating of two hulls dragged a fender down between the boats.

Crew should have one hand on the boat—especially when standing on an open deck. One surprise wake, and the girl standing next to the boom could find herself in the drink.

When cruising or racing, I tape lifeline shackles closed to ensure they will not open accidentally while on the open water.

Fenders should be tied to a cleat or to the base of stanchions and not, as here, to the stanchion tops or lifelines where they can exert leverage and cause damage.

To avoid trouble, tie fenders only to:

- The bases of your stanchions
- Cars on your jib track
- Cleats along the hull, or
- Openings in aluminum caprails.

The stanchions on my boat, a Pearson, are made with rings or loops at their base for the purpose of securing fenders.

When fenders are not in use, stow them in the lazarette or in stainless racks made for that purpose. Don't ride along with them dragging the water—they could work loose or lose their covers.

### Tip 1.7  Hazards of sitting on the pulpit or pushpit

Nothing could be more exhilarating than sitting on the pulpit (the front, or bow, railing) as witnessed in that memorable scene from the epic movie "*Titanic.*" Crewmembers also love to sit on the pushpit (the aft railing) of a boat—it provides a perfect vantage point from which to take in the whole nautical experience.

The pulpit and pushpit also provide perfect diving platforms for unscheduled backflips, followed by a view of the stern moving away into the distance. Falls from the pulpit, with the boat and propeller looming close behind, present an even greater hazard.

I am very firm in not allowing crew or guests to sit on any of the perimeter railings or lifelines.

## Tip 1.8 Practice crew-overboard rescues

Every once in a while, when my wife and I are out enjoying the sea, I'll quietly take one of our fenders, throw it overboard, and say (not yell) to my sailing (and life) mate, "Crew overboard!"

I don't do this for her benefit, I do it for mine, in case I ever go overboard. Guess who will be looking for a fast and skillful pickup?

I remember doing this during the practice run for a race on a friend's boat. We had a young crew aboard a 40-foot Santa Cruz practicing in Monterey Bay, California. Over went the fender, followed by the call, and what ensued was panic. In the 55°F water of the Pacific, the "crew overboard" expired from hypothermia long before being rescued. The skipper and I explained that the fender could have been one of them. Our crew, cocky as they were at first, then took it upon themselves to practice the drill until it was perfect.

Even though you may be boating in seas warmer than that, don't think you aren't at risk. Shock will hamper a victim's ability to think clearly and to actively participate in being pulled from the water.

You can't practice this drill enough. Use the guidelines below, adjusting them according to how many hands you have in your crew.

At the call "Crew overboard!":

1.  One crewmember immediately stands on deck and points to the person overboard and *continues to point* until the person is back on deck.

2.  The next person gets on the VHF radio and calls the Coast Guard. (Even if you are very lucky and are able to retrieve the person in the first few minutes, there is a high probability that you will need medical assistance. And if you are *not* lucky, you will have called for help early in the emergency.)

The alert call is "Pan-Pan" not "Mayday," since the vessel herself is not in danger (see Tip 4 8). Be ready to provide this information to the Coast Guard:

- The number of persons on board
- The status of your situation
- Your location, and
- The color and identifying features of your vessel.

3. If you're sailing and you have ancillary power, get the sails down immediately and start the engine. (If you are sailing and are the only one left on deck, loosen the sheets—the lines that control the sails—and let the sails flog. But don't let the lines out all the way. You must be careful of lines in the water that could get snagged in your prop during the rescue.)

    If you do not have power, you will need to tack back to the person in the water and be prepared to let all your sails luff (fly free) in time to glide to a stop at just the right moment. This takes practice—please do! As soon as you can safely do so, get the sails down. They will interfere with your ability to hold the vessel next to your victim

4. Throw anything that floats toward the victim. At the very least it will mark the spot, and it may be exactly the flotation the victim needs.

5. Allow no one to go in the water to help the victim. If you do, you will then have two or more persons overboard.

6. Get lines ready.

7. Come up to the victim with your vessel pointing *into the wind* so that you have control over boat speed and position. When you reach the victim, place your boat to windward of him or her so the wind and currents carry the boat toward the victim rather than away.

8. Once you're alongside the victim, put the engine in neutral but don't switch it off. You may have to go around again.

    Be exceedingly careful here: The fact that you are in neutral does not mean that your propeller is not turning. Make an effort well in advance to see if your propeller shaft turns when the gear is in neutral. If it does, you will need your wits about you at the time of an emergency. You will have to exercise great care when you come alongside your victim. In this case, be sure to keep the victim as far away from the propeller as possible at all times.

    If the victim needs to come up a stern ladder or platform, *turn the engine(s) off* as soon as you have a line firmly secured around the victim. When you need to move again, keep a sharp lookout for lines in the water.

9. Lifting the victim out of the water may be difficult. Remember that a person will weigh twice as much as normal in waterlogged clothing. Furthermore, fright and shock often will render the victim incapable of providing assistance. Even if your vessel has a ladder, your victim may not be able to use it.

    This situation calls for ingenuity. For example, you may be able to use the lines and sheaves (pulleys) from your dinghy davits, or your spinnaker halyard by working the free end of the line on a winch. Think about the process ahead of time and plan how you would deal with the situation should it ever occur. Some sailors keep a special four-part block-and-tackle ready for this very eventuality.

10. Once aboard, get the person below and remove all wet clothes immediately. Get dry clothes on. Keep the person warm even after he or she claims to be okay. Wrap your patient in warm blankets or jackets. If you have extra crew available, have them hug the victim to help build body temperature. Prepare a warm drink if you can. Even though your victim is aboard, do not assume he or she is okay until someone medically qualified has confirmed it.

11. Most important, review these rules with your crew ahead of time. You will not have the opportunity to grab this book in an emergency. Talk about your crew-overboard drill. Practice it. It is very serious business.

12. Stay calm.

## Tip 1.9  Have a horseshoe lifebuoy ready

Whenever you're on the water, you should always have a horseshoe lifebuoy or some form of life ring easily accessible, secured to the boat on a 100-foot line, and ready to be grabbed and thrown without untying, unclipping, or other delays. On a sailboat, the best place to mount a lifebuoy is somewhere along the pushpit.

On a cabin cruiser, a good arrangement is to have one horseshoe on the pushpit and one on the aft flybridge rail, from which the captain can throw it without having to come below. One end of the line should stay tied to the boat as you encircle the victim. One-and-a-half turns around the victim will allow you to stop the vessel and pull in the line to retrieve the buoy and your victim. Once you stop, remember to shift your transmission(s) to neutral. Review the steps in Tip 1.8, especially Tip 1.8.8.

Horseshoe buoys should be ready for immediate use. This one is tied to its support and may be hard to remove in an emergency.

## Tip 1.10 Practice using distress flares

You and your crew should be familiar with loading, cocking, aiming and firing a flare pistol before you ever *need* to do it. White meteor flares are made for practice purposes. Allow your crew to practice with them. White meteor flares or white lights can also be used to indicate your position (for collision avoidance).

However, be aware that firing red meteor flares is illegal except in emergencies.

Red handheld flares should also be carried on board. They are excellent for indicating your position as help arrives.

Even when shooting white practice flares, it is both a good idea and a courtesy for you to call the Coast Guard and advise them of your tests.

The ring buoy in this powerboat is conveniently close at hand for the skipper or anyone on deck.

## Tip 1.11 Make sure grabrails and attachments are solid

All handrails and gripping points on your vessel should be professionally attached and, when necessary, through-bolted. Few things are more hazardous than an after-market handrail that is unable to withstand the shock of an off-balance adult suddenly grabbing it.

If you have any such fittings on your vessel, it is better to remove them than to risk the consequences of having one come free when somebody lunges for it in desperation. During your routine maintenance visits, inspect the handrail attachments for tightly fastened bolts and non-rusted fittings.

### Tip 1.12  Be seen even when YOU can't see

In fog and poor visibility, a proper reflector provides a better "target" for other vessel's radar transmissions than does your vessel's fiberglass or wooden hull. Radar reflectors come in many varieties, but all of them do a good job of bouncing radar signals back to their source. Dollar for dollar, they're one of the best safety investments you can make. Reflectors are hauled aloft by any halyard or line. For best detection by another vessel's radar, the reflector should be as high as possible.

Most powerboats present a surface large enough to produce a good target. Even so, a reflector offers added assurance of being seen. On powerboats, reflectors should be positioned above the flybridge so as to be detected from all sides of the vessel.

Reflectors are a great idea for smaller powerboats such as the popular bassboats. In foggy conditions, when fishing is still a viable pastime, it is important for your boat to be detected by oncoming vessels who are plodding through the area on radar.

### Tip 1.13  Alcohol, fire, and water don't mix

Many boaters seem to feel that somehow, out there on the water, away from crowds, blind corners, and motorcycle cops, is an extra element of security that permits accelerated alcohol consumption. If you can imagine what damage a 2,500-pound car can do at 30 miles an hour, try to envision what a 12,000-pound boat can do at 6 knots with no brakes and limited steerage.

I enjoy a cold one as much as anybody does. But I also have vivid memories of other boaters who missed me by inches, or whose splintered boats I helped fend away from the dock, or whom I've seen drive over anchor and mooring lines, because their eyes were redder than their running lights. So I make a practice of leaving my cold ones on ice until *after* my boat is anchored for the night.

Similarly, I don't allow smoking, above or below deck. Too risky. A fire on the water poses a serious threat to everyone on board when the only salvation is to head for the water. You're familiar with the phrase about being caught "between the Devil and the deep blue sea"? Enough said.

### Tip 1.14  Watch your wake

You are responsible for your wake. As a matter of courtesy, you should always be conscious of the effect of your vessel's wake on other boaters, water skiers, or anyone else nearby. As a matter of law, if the impact of your wake causes injury or damage it's *your* responsibility, whether there are no-wake signs posted or not.

You are responsible for your wake. The wake from this boat, which is passing too close to the photographer's boat, could inflict injury to a passenger on a neighboring vessel caught unawares.

If you've ever been knocked off your feet by the sudden smack of somebody else's wake, you know the potential for trouble. A few years ago, a friend jokingly ran a circle around me with his powerboat. Someone on my boat was hurt. It wasn't a joke. Don't inflict that experience on someone else.

## Tip 1.15 Do unto others . . .

The rules say that if you're near a vessel in distress, and you fail to come to its aid, you may be found negligent and be subject to fines. Aside from the rules, it's your duty as a skipper to help a fellow skipper in trouble. Just be sure to do it safely.

When the Coast Guard announces that "all vessels in the vicinity are requested to keep a sharp lookout . . ." that's not just silly chatter. If you hear the Coast Guard, or another station talking to a vessel in distress, listen. Discover the vessel's location. Go to her aid if it is possible.

When you come alongside, make sure that both vessels are protected by fenders, and that no crew or passengers are in jeopardy. If you tow another vessel, use as long a line as possible, to help absorb shocks. Towing speeds should not exceed 5 to 6 knots, and powerboaters should be aware that the average sailboat cannot be moved through the water faster than 8 knots.

Finally, work out with your tow *ahead of time* how, when, and where you will cast off your lines and just who will do what after that.

# Chapter 2

# NAVIGATION

It was about 8:30 A.M. when we pushed back from the dock and slid into the thin gray fog. We weren't about to lose a sailing day just because the race committee had called it quits. I was to be part of a wedding party at 1 P.M. and an hour's sail was a fantastic way to start an otherwise bleak day.

Stuart's *Celebrity* was a sleek day-sailer. Her mahogany hull was sparsely fitted with just the right gear for the sailing purist. Absent a motor, VHF, loran, or even a compass, we bobbed through the mist, contemplating our decision to leave. We knew Lake Hoptacong like the backs of our hands, but in the fog, even to an invincible chartless sailor, it all looked the same. Again and again we attempted to find our starting point. At around 4 P.M. the fog lifted like a giant curtain and, much to our surprise, we found ourselves only 30 feet from the dock.

## Tip 2.1 Be chart smart

Sailing safely requires being familiar with the charted *aids to navigation*, the representations of underwater hazards and known water depths. This information has been set down for you, in detail, on widely available charts (the marine equivalent of shoreside maps). There is no excuse for venturing anywhere with your boat and crew if you don't have a clue about the dangers that lie beneath the water's surface. Buy the charts that cover the areas where you'll be boating, and study them thoroughly before you leave the dock.

Charts come in four basic types:

1. Standard paper charts produced by government agencies.

2. Plastic-coated charts produced by private companies.

3. Chart books (covering specific regions) that usually include some historical background, marina information, and points of interest.

4. Digital charts used in GPS and loran chart plotters.

Choose any type that suits your taste, your budget and the size of your navigation table. All marine paper charts have revision dates printed in the lower margins. Yours should have the most recent dating.

Charts should be used only for reference. Never consider them to be guaranteed sources of information, no matter how official they look. Many current charts contain survey data that are several decades old, gathered with leadline and sextant. Even if you have the most recently dated chart, bottom conditions can change rapidly. Shorelines and landmarks sometimes change, too, lights go out, and markers are knocked down. You must consider other measurements and observations before you assume your navigational data are accurate.

Charts contain data about objects on shore (towers, major buildings, smokestacks, and so on), the position and names of buoys (see Tip 2.6), and a grid system that provides the latitude and longitude for everything on the chart. Latitude and longitude are measured in degrees, minutes, and seconds (or hundredths of a minute, according to the system you are using). Therefore, the display of minutes can be in increments of 10, 60, or 100.

One degree of latitude equals 60 nautical miles, each minute equals one nautical mile (a nautical mile is 6,076 feet), and if we are using the decimal convention for increments of a minute, ⅒th of a minute equals 607 feet. You can calculate these distances from degrees and minutes when working on a chart. For example, if one line of *latitude* on your chart says

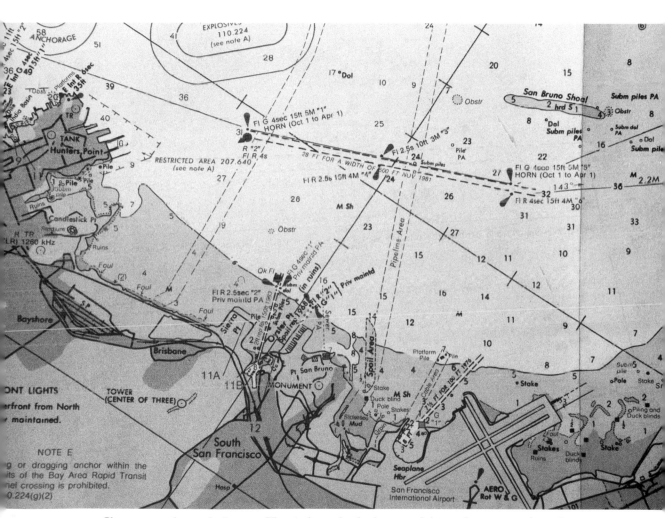

Charts are road maps for boaters. They indicate depths, buoys and day marks, marinas, channels, and bottom conditions. They also point out important landmarks.

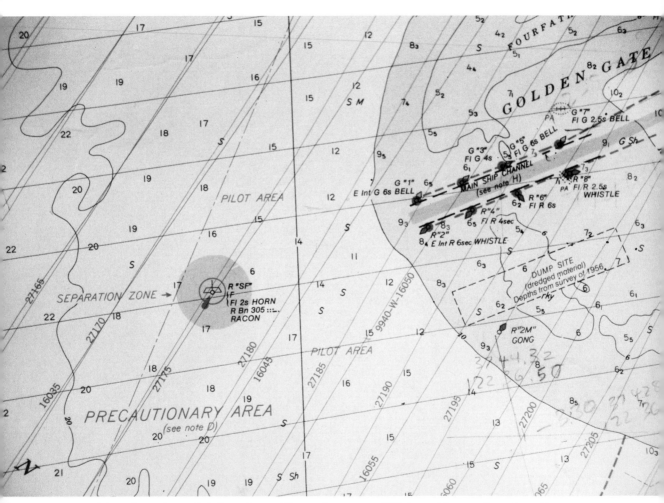

Many charts also include loran "time difference" overprints (TDs), in addition to latitude and longitude. Loran uses TD information as the core data to derive its latitude and longitude computations. TDs are not used for GPS navigation.

40°22' (forty degrees, twenty-two minutes) and the next one says 40°20' (a difference of two minutes), you know they are two miles apart.

Distances can be measured only from tick marks on the lines running North/South or latitude scales which appear in the margins of the chart. Since lines of longitude get closer together as they near the North or South Poles, distance measurements should not be taken from tick marks on lines running East and West on the chart.

When using a loran or GPS receiver (see Tip 2.11, Choose high-tech help wisely), most systems display the increments of lat/long (latitude and longitude) to two decimal places or 100th of a minute—that's equivalent to 60 feet (there are 6,076 feet in a nautical mile, 607 feet to ⅒th of a mile, and 60 feet to ⅟₁₀₀th of a mile).

Better systems allow you to select between the seconds or hundredths display. Trimble Navigation, one of the earliest providers of high-quality loran and GPS systems, made equipment that displayed increments of minutes to three decimal places. Thus, the last digit equaled steps of six feet. The use of three decimal places was not to suggest that the device could display *absolute* latitude and longitude accuracy to six feet, but rather that its potential for *repeatable* accuracy (getting to the same place twice) was reasonably good.

So, if you were sitting outside the harbor at San Juan, Puerto Rico, your loran or GPS might read (according to your exact position): 18° 30'10" N, 66° 07' 20" W.

Now: Can you determine what the difference is between these two latitude indications: 48° 20' 06" and 48° 21' 06"?

(If you guessed one nautical mile, you are correct.)

How about these two: 40° 20' 06" and 40° 20' 10"?

(You should have answered 404 feet. The difference was four seconds. Each second is 101 feet (6,076/60=101), and four times 101 is 404.)

If you are working on a system that provides hundredths of a minute, you might encounter these two readings: 40° 20' 06 and 40° 20' 10. What is the difference in this example? You should have answered 240 feet. The difference was four 100ths of a minute. Since each 10th is 607 feet, then each 100th is 60 feet, and four times 60 is 240.

One important addition to your on-board library should be copies of the Coast Guard's "Local Notices To Mariners." These newsletter-format mailings come out weekly and contain valuable up-to-date information on navigational hazards (buoys destroyed or moved, extinguished lights, drilling rigs or dredges working in specific areas, and so forth), marine events (such as races, regattas, and military operations) and relevant loran and GPS operational information. "Local Notices to Mariners" are available free, but you must order them anew at the beginning of each year. A subscription renewal questionnaire is provided on the back page of each issue during the month of December. For information about subscribing to your local version, call the regional office of the Coast Guard and ask for either the Local Notice or Traffic Safety office.

Most charts are printed with north at the top, east to the right, west to the left, and south at the bottom. All charts include at least one compass rose, a circle showing the points of the compass. Each compass rose comprises two circles: The outer one is the true compass rose, with a north indicator pointing directly to the geographic North Pole. The inner circle is the magnetic compass rose. In most locations, the two compasses do not agree. For example, a chart of New York harbor will show the north pointer of the magnetic (inner) compass rose pointing about 11 degrees west of true north. This difference is called the variation, abbreviated "var." Somewhere around the Mississippi, the two compass roses will be aligned and have no variation. And, along the Californian coast, the magnetic compass will have a variation of about 12 degrees east. This phenomenon is caused by the earth's magnetic field, the north pole of which is near, but not at, the geographic North Pole (this is why your magnetic compass does not point to true north).

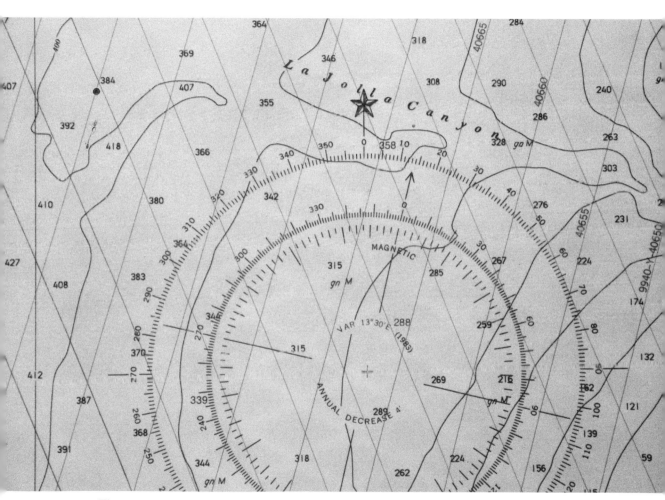

The most important symbol on a marine chart is the compass rose. The north indicator on the outer circle points to true north (the geographic North Pole). The north indicator on the inner circle points to magnetic north.

To give you another idea of how the variation differs, a 1994 chart of the Lesser Antilles (Puerto Rico to Martinique) showed a magnetic variation at the western end of Puerto Rico of 10° 40' west. To the east of Martinique, the variation was 14° 20' west.

Your compass heading is the direction in which you're traveling, as indicated by your steering compass. To transfer that heading to your chart, imagine that you are in the middle of the chart's compass rose looking out at the corresponding compass number on the inside circle (the magnetic compass rose).

To find your actual line of travel, you first need to know your precise location (see Tip 2.11, Choose high-tech help wisely).

You can obtain your location from loran or GPS, or by taking bearings from objects on land. Mark your location on the chart—in pencil only, please. Now, draw a line through your location that parallels your heading line on the compass rose. That new line is your heading. The chart now reveals the territory and possible hazards you will traverse if you continue along your line.

Deviation is another phenomenon you need to understand when working with compasses. Deviation is the difference between any accurate magnetic direction and what your compass actually indicates. The offset is usually caused by some magnetic interference on the boat such as nearby metal or electrical wiring, or the failure of the compass to be fully compensated (adjustments made with magnets internal to the compass housing). Even after a compass has been "swung" (turned through many headings and corrected for the local magnetic interference), there still may be points around the compass where the needle or dome cannot be made to agree with one or more accurate bearings. For example, your compass might be perfectly aligned in all points in the northern, western, and southern quadrants, but when you are heading east, the compass needle might have a deviation of 4 degrees north or south. To know your true headings for all points of your compass, you can prepare a deviation card, which is simply a listing of 36 bearings, 10 degrees apart (totaling 360 degrees). It indicates how your compass behaves relative to the accurate magnetic bearings. (Fewer—six or eight—bearings may be adequate.)

In popular tourist regions, local establishments often duplicate segments of marine charts for promotional purposes (place mats, tablecloths, and so forth). These charts should never be used for navigation since they are rarely up to date, typically have critical information omitted or obscured and are occasionally modified to satisfy graphic needs.

## Tip 2.2  Know where "here" is

Not long ago I monitored a radio call from a vessel in distress. The call to Coast Guard Group San Francisco came from a 37-foot sailboat that was drifting without power and without enough wind to sail. The crew had experienced an engine fire and extinguished it. Now the skipper was afraid to restart the engine. Fortunately they still had battery power, and he was calling for help.

Unfortunately, nobody aboard the vessel had any idea where they were. That first call went out at about 1800 (6 P.M.) and it wasn't until 2030 (8:30 P.M.) that the Coast Guard finally located them after a great effort. Two-and-a-half hours waiting to be found—and they were in a virtually landlocked bay.

It makes no sense to sail or power along in complete ignorance of your position. If you run into a major problem, as that sailboat did, or if someone aboard your vessel becomes seriously ill, you can't pull into a gas station to ask directions. Have charts aboard, and refer to them.

Long-distance cruisers and diligent racers keep an ongoing log of their positions. Aside from knowing their distance made good, in the event they lose all power, they have an accurate idea of their last known location.

If you need help learning to read charts, there are plenty of navigation courses available through yacht clubs, the Coast Guard Auxiliary, and sailing schools.

It now costs very little to have loran, or GPS, or both, aboard. These devices can describe your position to such accuracy that you can tell another boater or the Coast Guard where you are to within 150 feet. With the help of your charts, they will also help you locate your position relative to nearby harbors and hazards. You'll be warned about shallow water, and you'll be able to find favorite anchorages and fishing holes. (See Tip 2.11, Choose high-tech help wisely.)

## Tip 2.3  Know the tides

In some parts of the world, tidal changes and the currents that accompany them are severe enough to present a threat to boaters. Along much of the eastern seaboard of the U.S., tides ebb and flow serenely, producing a change in water level of no more than a few feet. But in places with extensive channels, bays, and fairways (San Francisco Bay, for instance) the change can be dramatic: six feet and more, with greater ranges found in estuaries where the morphology of the basin exaggerates the tidal changes, causing low lows and high highs. Currents in such areas can be swift and formidable, causing choppy water and creating hazardous eddies around rocks, pilings, and other objects. In these areas, mooring to a non-floating dock or quay at high tide can lead to a very embarrassing, and possibly disastrous, end at low tide.

But there's no reason to be surprised by tidal effects, anywhere. You can pick up free local tide tables or buy books with easy-to-follow tidal charts that cover any place you're apt to visit with your boat. Since the times of high and low tides are different every day, this year's tables are not usable next year. New tide tables should appear on the shelves of your local marine or fishing shop each November or early December.

These books conveniently list the times and heights of low tide and high tide and the times and strengths of maximum tidal currents (which are not the same as the times for low tide and high tide) at the reference stations where data have been compiled and calculations made. Other locations are given relative to the nearest reference stations. For example, you might find that at the location of interest to you, on the date and time you'll be there, high water will be 11 minutes later, and low water 15 minutes later, than at the designated reference station.

Tide tables may also provide the times of slack water, the point where there is no horizontal movement of water either on the ebb or the flood tide. In estuaries and large bays, the times of slack water do not always correspond with times of high or low water, though they are usually fairly close.

Unless you boat exclusively on lakes, get tide tables for the areas where you'll be boating, and study them—before you go—as carefully as you study your charts.

## Tip 2.4  Make the tides work for you

Ever take an airline flight that landed early because it picked up a tail wind? In the same way, keeping track of tides can help you make better time on inland waters. For example, if you're in an estuary, heading inland at 6 knots, and doing so in the middle of a 2-knot flood (incoming) tide, then your actual speed over the ground is 8 knots. On the other hand, if you try the same trip at the same power in the middle of a 2-knot ebb (outgoing) tide, you will make just 4 knots over ground—only half as fast. It's like trying to walk up the down escalator.

That's another reason you should make it a habit to check tide tables as part of your preparation for any trip. It's well worth the effort, and will help you select the ideal time for your departure. It will also help you estimate the time en route to your destination.

## Tip 2.5  Know WHERE to look when you're estimating currents

Many skippers estimate the strength of current flow by the angle at which they see navigation buoys leaning. Many are fooled.

In some cases, buoys don't lean in the direction of the current, but instead lean the opposite way. Here's why: The current flow against the buoy's anchor chain, working in concert with the natural tendency of the buoy to right itself, pushes the lower portion of the buoy in the direction of the current, while the upper portion tilts back upstream. This phenomenon is common, for example, on San Francisco Bay. The tendency for this tilting differs with the construction of the buoy, so don't base assumptions on the angle you see. You're better off judging the current flow by looking at the ripples or eddy streaming from the buoy.

Navigation buoys don't always lean in the direction of the current. Here, the current can clearly be seen flowing to the right while the buoy leans to the left.

## Tip 2.6  Know your way around the buoyage system

Inland waterways, including bays, estuaries, rivers, and lakes, are carefully posted with channel markers and buoys. They provide vital information about bottom conditions (shallow depths or hazardous outcroppings) that could hamper your ability to pass, and they are important aids when you're going from location to location.

There are two basic types, red markers and green markers, that designate channels and fairways, and a series of two-color buoys that mark special points, such as mid-channel or "separation buoys." Sometimes you'll see older black markers instead of green ones, though these are being phased out. When you're under way, red markers are always to be passed to the right as you're returning from sea or moving upstream. (The preferred phrasing for that is "leave them to starboard.") Memorize the phrase "Red Right Returning."

Aids to navigation, such as this red-light buoy, provide reliable "landmarks" for boaters; but the rules of buoy coloring and numbering must be well understood.

Aside from the two sea lions grabbing some afternoon sun, note the difference between the buoy in this picture and the buoy in the previous picture. One is triangular and the other square, but both are even-numbered. The shape rule cannot always be applied to floating lighted buoys. Triangular markers (typically point up) are red and even-numbered. The wedge-shaped pockets at the top of this marker are radar reflectors.

Green markers should be left on your left (port) side when you're returning from sea. Naturally, when you're heading out to sea, the green markers should be to the right (the starboard side). Whenever there's any ambiguity, the chart is the final arbiter.

Markers are numbered in sequence for their area. This helps you locate them on charts, and helps you track your progress through a chan-

Each aspect of marker recognition (shape, color, and numbering) is important. With the sun behind this daymark, we can't see its color or number but the square shape tells us that it must be green and odd-numbered and should be kept to port when returning from sea.

nel. Red markers always have even numbers; green markers have odd numbers. Both kinds of markers may carry lights or radar reflectors; buoys may also carry sound devices such as bells or horns.

Besides coming in two colors, markers come in two shapes: triangular and square. Red markers are triangular or conical, green markers are square or cylindrical.

There are also several types of markers: daymarks (or day beacons), which are mounted on posts permanently affixed to the bottom in shallower water; and buoys, which are anchored by a chain to a weight on the seabed. Daymarks are always in the same position, but a buoy can swing on its anchor chain and, depending on the water depth and current, could be floating as far as a quarter mile from its charted location.

In some rivers and lakes, molded plastic buoys are common. Note that this lighted green marker is cylindrical (which appears square) and odd-numbered. Without a light, the cylindrical green buoy would be called a "can" and an unlit red triangular buoy would be called a "nun."

This buoy is red and conical (which appears triangular) and though we can't see its number, we know it must be even. Keep it to starboard when going upstream or returning from the sea.

This navigation system is used in lake regions as well, where the "returning from sea" rule seems to have no bearing. It is important to remember, however, that you must stay between the markers regardless of whether red is "left" or "right." Also, in most lake regions, you will find many private markers, some as simple as bleach bottles secured with a line. Respect these markers as well. They are there as a warning and indicate everything from "rocks below" to "stay clear of my boathouse."

Less sophisticated buoys are found in unpopulated regions. This isolated, simple buoy guides boaters to safe passage. Even though this cone is small and unsophisticated, it is still red and triangular.

Separation buoys are multicolored. This red/green buoy is a preferred channel marker whose top-most red barrel suggests the preferred channel is to port. It is one of many that mark the center of the channel in the Chesapeake-Delaware Canal.

For quick reference, here's a summary of the basics about buoys and channel markers:

- Red markers should always be kept to your right when you're re-turning from sea (that is, heading inland or upstream). Remember the rule "Red, Right, Returning." Red markers are even-numbered (2, 4, 6, etc.) and usually are triangular in shape. Whenever it's uncertain as to which direction constitutes "returning from sea," consult your chart. Better yet, consult your chart anyway.

- Green markers (or sometimes, black ones) should always be kept to your left when you're returning from sea. Green markers are odd-numbered (1, 3, 5, etc.), and usually are square in shape.

- Bi-colored markers (black/red, black/white, and so on) typically mark turning points or the center of a channel. Usually they are identified by letters rather than by numbers, and are referred to as "separation buoys" or "separation markers." Some two-color markers, also bearing letters instead of numbers, indicate other reference or meeting points, such as a place where seagoing vessels pick up local pilots. (In most major harbors, pilots are sent to board vessels to assist in guiding vessels safely into ports and through difficult channels.)

The color, the shape, and the numbering system are all important. For example, sometimes in fog, you can just make out the shape of a buoy but can't determine its color or its number. Other times, at night, your flashlight might be able to pick up the reflective color but you can't see the number or the shape. Take a minute to memorize "RET" (red, even, triangular) and "SOG" (square, odd, green).

## Tip 2.7  Missing markers may mean trouble

If a daymark (an aid to navigation that is mounted on a post or piling) is missing from its indicated position, steer well clear of the spot, favoring the deep-water side. The piling may be down and submerged, just below the waterline, and could pose a serious threat to you and your vessel. (One more good reason to know your chart.)

In general, remember there is always the chance of finding a light out or a buoy missing (perhaps knocked down by a tanker or a tug). So never rely on markers as your sole references for navigation.

Occasionally, aids are mixed. Here a floating buoy replaces a destroyed daymark.

## Tip 2.8 Understand what charts tell you about markers

On charts, aids to navigation are marked with specific symbols. Beneath the symbol is a dot that shows the designated location of the aid. An accompanying notation gives details about the function of the buoy or marker there. These notations are in navigational shorthand, so you want to be familiar with what the different abbreviations mean.

Chart symbols and abbreviations are explained in detail in a booklet published by the Defense Mapping Agency (DMA). It is called *Chart No. 1, United States of America*, and carries illustrated descriptions of all nautical chart symbols, terms, and abbreviations. It carries the DMA stock number WOBZC1. Though it may not be a killer title, get this book. It is available at most chandlers or boating-goods stores.

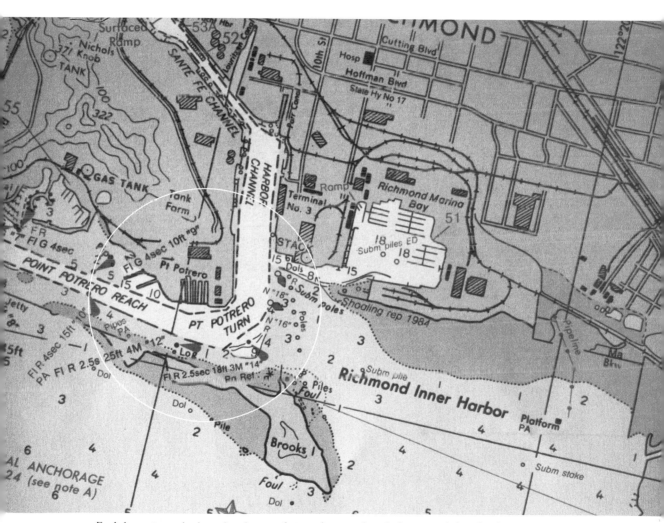

Each buoy is marked on the chart with its color, number, light interval, height above water at low tide (unless it is a floating buoy), and distance at which its light can be seen.

A complete discussion of chart symbols and abbreviations is beyond the scope of this book, but the pointers below should give you the general idea. Most U.S. charts show measurements in feet and miles, and the measurement scheme is clearly marked in large letters along the edge of all charts. Charts showing soundings (depths) in fathoms (6 feet equal 1 fathom) are clearly marked. (Note: As of February 1993, the measurement standard of the National Ocean Survey [NOS], which is part of the National Oceanic and Atmospheric Administration [NOAA], was officially changed to the metric system. Over time, existing charts will be superseded by new charts with metric measurements, but that's likely to be a slow process.) Here are some examples of buoy notations, along with translations of the navigationese:

**Fl R 4sec 15ft 3M "6"**

This aid is a flashing red daymark with a light interval of 4 seconds. (That is, from the time it begins to flash until the next time it begins to flash— or from the time the light goes out until the next time the light goes out— is a period of 4 seconds.) It stands 15 feet above the water at mean high tide. The light is visible for 3 miles, and the mark is numbered 6.

How do we know this is a daymark? Daymarks always are described with their heights above water at mean high tide. Buoys are always the same height above the water on which they float, so no such reference is necessary.

**"1" Fl G 6sec**

This aid is a buoy (there is no reference to its height above water). It is numbered 1, and it has a flashing green light with a period of 6 seconds.

Incidentally, in both of our examples so far, the marker is painted the same color as the light.

## Qk Fl G "1"

This is a quick-flashing light, a designation that usually means it flashes 60 times per minute. Now, based on what you've already learned, is it a daymark or a floating buoy? What is its color? What is its number? (You're right! It is green because it says "G.") We also know it is green because it is odd-numbered. And it is buoy number 1.

Here are some other symbols you may find next to a charted aid:

| | |
|---|---|
| C | Can or cylindrical buoy (usually green, odd-numbered). |
| N | Nun or conical buoy (usually red, even-numbered). |
| SP | Spherical buoy. |
| BELL | Just what it says. |
| GONG | Just what it says. |
| WHIS | Whistle. |

Here are some common color notations:

| | |
|---|---|
| GR | Green-and-red horizontal bands, with the green band on top; the preferred channel is to starboard. |
| RG | Red-and-green horizontal bands, with the red band on top; the preferred channel is to port. |
| RB | Red-and-black. |
| BR | Black-and-red. |

If all you see next to a symbol's dot on the chart is "1," you can properly assume that it is a number 1 buoy, and because it is odd, it is green (or possibly black), and it should be left to port when returning from sea.

One final word on lights. As well as having different periods (3sec, 5sec, etc.), lights stay on for different durations of time to help you keep track of the buoy you are timing. While two buoys may have five-second periods, for example, the lights may stay on for two seconds on one buoy and three seconds on another. The Coast Guard takes great care in planning the location of buoys so that lights of the same interval will not be in sight of one another. In some cases, however, the need for numerous navigation buoys may dictate a few buoys' having the same interval (which requires that you know more about your location than just buoy verification). In the approach to New York from the Long Island Sound, for example, the number of buoys is so great that some intervals have to be repeated. Of course, you still must know which one you are looking at, based on your dead-reckoning position and the location of other aids to navigation.

## Tip 2.9 Know who has the right of way, and never argue

On the water, the equivalent of the automobile Vehicle Code is the *International Regulations for Preventing Collisions at Sea* (Colregs). Strictly speaking, the international regulations apply to situations on the high seas and outer coastal waters. Those of us who cruise U.S. inner coastal or inland waters are subject to the *Inland Navigational Rules of the United States* (the "inland rules" for short). But for all practical purposes, the two codes were unified in 1982.

The rules clearly define all the situations in which one vessel should give way to another. But they also list one overriding rule:

*No matter who has the legal right of way, it is the duty of each skipper to avoid collision at all costs.*

Know the regulations well enough to understand what is expected of you, and what courtesies you should show other boaters. Even when the rules say you're in the right, be 100 percent ready to abandon your course and do what it takes to get out of a bad situation safely. That's common sense.

When meeting head-on, it is important for each skipper to know the other's intentions. You should pass port-to-port, but doing so, as in this case, is not always practical. Make your intentions known by turning your boat early.

Here's an example: Boaters often get on a soapbox about the rule that supposedly states: "Sailboats have the right of way over power vessels." True? Not without a lot of caveats.

First, a sailboat is only considered a "sailing vessel" under the rules when she is powered by sail alone; if her sails are up *and* her engine is running, she is "power-driven." A sailing vessel has right of way over a power-driven vessel *unless* the latter is engaged in fishing that affects her ability to maneuver, is constrained by her draft, or is restricted in her ability to maneuver for any other reason. And, according to little-known Rule 13, a sailing vessel must always give way to any power-driven vessel she overtakes.

When passing, the sailboat rules apply. Here the sailboat on the port tack (from which the photo was taken) must stay clear of the sailboat on the starboard tack.

Then there's the matter of common sense. A large vessel entering or exiting a congested harbor, even in the hands of a pilot and with a lookout at the bow, cannot maneuver effectively enough to avoid a collision with a small vessel whose skipper thinks it can cross in time or feels it has the "right of way." The helmsman and assisting pilot of a small tanker can't see anything low down on the water 800 to 1,000 feet directly in front. Further, communication with a lookout at the bow takes time and must be precise. Don't make assumptions about your speed, your privileges, or ability to be seen. Right of way or not, if you can't be seen, you can't be avoided

I doubt that most San Francisco and Hudson River sailboaters realize these waterways are considered a *narrow channel or fairway*. That means sailboats must keep clear of powered vessels using the traffic separation schemes.

Finally, the idea of a "right of way" itself fell out of favor after much abuse and subsequent court cases. Instead, we now speak of the *stand-on* vessel and the *give-way* vessel. The rules prescribe each skipper's obligations when two vessels meet.

You should be familiar with the stipulations of the Colregs, but here are four rules of thumb that will help you in most situations. Just remember that following any rules blindly, without allowing for the unexpected, could lead to disaster. Use common sense and, of course, don't make any assumptions.

- If you are under power, the powered vessel crossing from your right to your left is the stand-on vessel. You are the give-way vessel.

- You should signal your intention to pass behind the crossing vessel by turning your boat to the right. As she continues across the line of your original course, you can turn to resume your

Powerboats should pass with enough sea room to avoid causing problems with their wakes. At night, if you are passing properly, you should see each other's port (red) light.

original course and pass astern of (behind) her. *Caution:* Be careful of her wake and always look to be sure the crossing vessel isn't towing something. (This is not a joke: some tugs in open water have tows a quarter mile behind them.)

When you meet another powerboat head-to-head, pass port-to-port. In this sense, boating is like driving a car in the U.S. When you approach another vessel head-on or nearly so, turn to the right early and make clear your intention to pass port-side-to-port-side. Obviously, if you find yourself in a situation where it would make more sense to pass starboard-to-starboard, and you have enough sea room, do so. Don't make an awkward course change just to follow the letter of the rule. In either case, be sure to make your intentions clear by positioning your boat early. And, of course, do not take it for granted that the other skipper understands your intention. By all means, do not assume that the other vessel even sees you. Monitor the approaching vessel's course.

Overtaking vessels can pass on either side but should give a warning signal beforehand. One short blast on the horn means "I intend to overtake you on your starboard side," and two short blasts means "I intend to overtake you on your port side." Steaming down the Delaware River, the closer of these two vessels gave us little warning or time to get out of her way and . . .

● Powerboats should yield to sailboats under most circumstances. Powerboaters should note that the impact of their wakes can cause a serious injury to someone on a sailboat. Give sailboats a wide berth. Sailboaters should take nothing for granted. Steer clear of powerboats, and turn to cross their wakes at right angles.

. . . without signaling, passes much too close for comfort.

This tug was on its way to do some business in a hurry. Since we were heading toward the right of the picture, we were the stand-on vessel. The tug, the give-way vessel, soon turned to starboard to indicate its intention to pass clear behind us.

Stay well clear of tugs towing barges. Tugs often pull their tows at a great distance; the cables are often invisible and the path of the tow can be difficult to ascertain. Barges in tow are especially difficult to spot when it's dark, and you must be fully familiar with the lighting scheme of tugs if you plan to go boating at night.

●   Colregs contain specific rules for sailboats. Here is a quick extract of rules 9(b), 10(j), 12, and 13: A sailboat should not impede another vessel that can only navigate safely in a narrow channel or fairway or one that is following a traffic lane. When two sailboats meet, whether racing or not, sailboats on a port tack (wind coming over the port side) should keep out of the way of sailboats on opposite tacks (if in doubt of the other's tack, the vessel on the port tack should still stay clear). If both sailboats are on the same tack, the one that is windward (the side opposite to where the mainsail is) should keep out of the way of the other boat. When one vessel is overtaking another, the overtaking vessel should stay well clear of the vessel being overtaken.

●   Note that the rules do not address situations involving more than two vessels. When you find yourself in such a circumstance, deal with one situation at a time and let common sense be your guide. When a collision occurs, *everyone* is at fault.

### Tip 2.10  Use your eyes, ears, and antennae

When the regulations say you should use *all means possible to avoid a collision*, they're talking about a lot more than the maneuvers you make when another boat happens to get too close. The words "all means possible" are the key here.

You're expected always to have someone on watch. If you have a VHF radio, you should have it on and be monitoring Channel 16 (the calling and emergency channel). If you have radar, you should have it on and be watching it. If you have a loran or GPS receiver, it must be on and you should be monitoring it so that you know where you are, and whether your vessel is in a major traffic lane.

If you aren't using everything at your disposal to be aware and safe, you aren't living up to the rules of the road. If something happens, you could be found guilty just for not having a piece of equipment turned on.

Keep a sharp lookout for flotsam in the water, especially after heavy storms. Logs, sticks, plastic bags, and other debris can find their way to your prop or to your engine's water intake and destroy an otherwise pleasant voyage. More importantly, don't assume that every diver knows to fly a "divers down" flag (red flag with white diagonal stripe or international code flag A [blue and white swallowtail])—another reason not to pass too close to other boats.

Keep a sharp lookout. This vessel's visibility is reduced by the jetty. After speeding out of the channel, she could face unexpected company beyond the mouth of the inlet.

Small shoreside signs warn of cable crossings, hazardous anchorages, and so on. Take the time to read them—underwater cables *will* find your anchor.

Keep your eyes on the water, too. Sea lions and dolphins can get out of your way, but scuba divers and swimmers are much less agile.

Here's another good reason to watch the water: floating debris seems to be magnetically attracted to spinning propellers.

## Tip 2.11  Choose high-tech help wisely

What electronic navigational aid gives you the most help for your money: Loran-C? Global Positioning System (GPS)? Radar? Satellite Navigation (satnav)?

This question has been argued for years, and comes up in every navigation class I teach. I'm not going to try to make up your mind for you. But perhaps I can help you make a more informed choice.

Loran-C, which homes in on land-based radio beacons, is a superb coastal navigational tool. A good Loran-C system with a properly mounted antenna will guide you into any harbor in the coastal or inland waters of the United States. Loran offers a "repeatable" accuracy (finding the same spot twice) of about 200 feet (the best and most expensive systems get that

While the future of loran is seriously jeopardized by GPS, it still provides excellent 24-hour coastal accuracy to well within 100 feet.

down to about 75 feet) and does a great job from the Florida Keys to the tip of Maine, and from Alaska to as far south as Ensenada, Mexico; but outside its range, you're on your own. Loran also provides Time Difference (TD) information (the difference in transmission times to your position from the loran stations) if you like to use that data to plot your fixes.

The loran lines on most navigation charts are TDs and indicate the difference in microseconds of signals from two or more loran towers. The computer in the loran receiver measures the TDs and computes the latitude and longitude. Loran is still operational across the entire U.S. but the Hawaiian loran chain was recently shut down in favor of GPS. Although the whole loran system is maintained by the U.S. Coast Guard, it might not be for much longer. The system might be dismantled after the turn of the century.

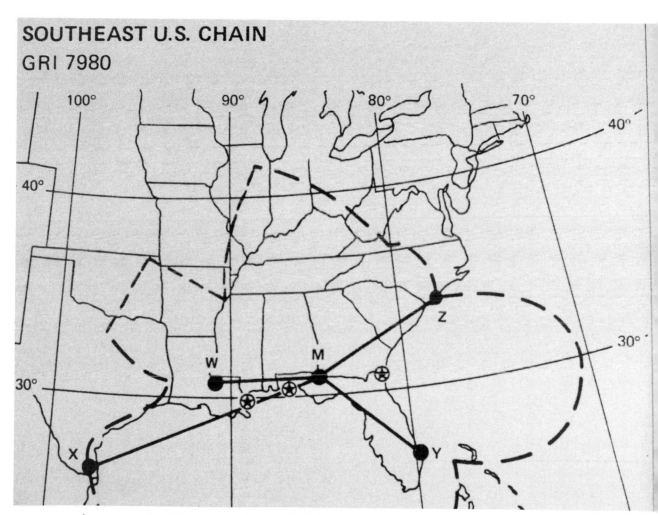

Loran users should become familiar with GRIs (group repetition intervals) to know where the best and worst coverage areas are.

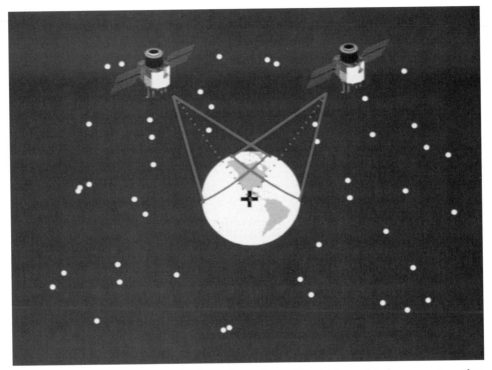

GPS satellites are in a 55° equatorial orbit and provide excellent 24-hour global coverage to within 50 feet.

A GPS unit, which relies on signals from orbiting satellites that are 11,000 nautical miles above the earth, is good anywhere in the world. The system relies on six "constellations" of three satellites each (the entire system consists of the 18, plus a couple of "spares") for 24-hour coverage. Its accuracy (depending on how many channels the receiver has and the logic of its circuitry) can be better than that of loran, typically giving you a position fix to within 50 feet.

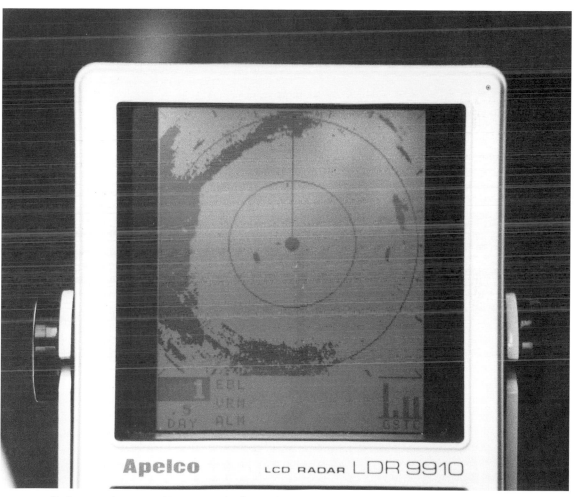

Radar provides an excellent eye in the fog or dark, and units are available for every size and type of boat. This small but efficient LCD screen provides excellent images with ranges from ¼ mile to 10 nautical miles.

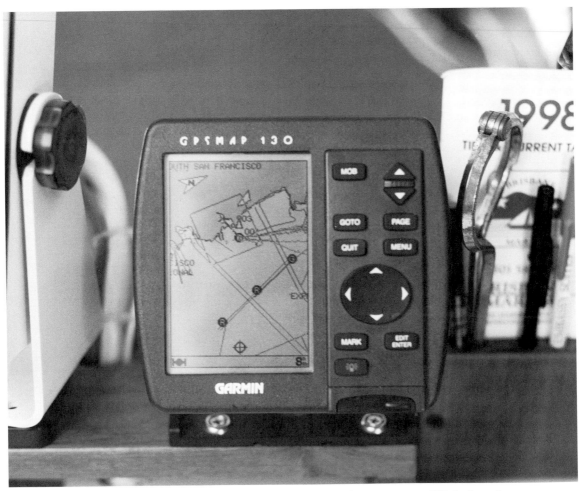

GPS and loran systems are available with excellent built-in charting systems. While these devices do not display what danger might be in front of you, as radar does, they do position your vessel on a chart with the accompanying buoys, depths, and land masses.

Single-channel receivers work well but multichannel systems provide a more reliable fix, since each channel is relegated to a specific signal-receiving task. Unlike loran, GPS is not affected by local radio interference, electric "noise" from bridges, or severe weather. Furthermore, GPS is becoming as cheap as loran. High-level "differential" GPS (DGPS) equipment, when used in conjunction with a land-based transmitter, can produce accuracies of one centimeter. If you can afford your boat, it should not be without GPS. GPS is maintained by the Department of Defense.

Neither loran nor GPS is a replacement for radar, and vice versa. Position indicating systems such as loran, GPS, and satnav (GPS's predecessor) tell you where you are, but don't tell you what is actually around you or heading toward you. Radar tells you where you are relative to other objects (vessels, buoys, and land masses), but doesn't put the information into a context for positional navigation as it relates to latitude and longitude. If the radar screen shows recognizable land masses and buoys, you can find your approximate position on a chart. But if you don't know what you're seeing, or if you're far from land, you will have no position reference. That's why position-indicating systems and radar should be used together.

When satnav was all we had, it was wonderful. This navigation system used signals from satellites in polar orbits (they went around the earth crossing over the North and South Pole). While satnav was reasonably accurate anywhere in the world, the onboard system took a long time to acquire the first fix (sometimes up to four hours). But, the issue is moot. Satnav has been phased out and coastal skippers should seriously consider making the transition to GPS. Satnav receivers make wonderful conversation pieces and bookends.

In making your choice, consider the size of your vessel, the availability of electric power, and the geographic area in which you go boating. Make your choice based on how often you experience fog, whether you go boating at night, if the body of water you boat in ever puts you out of sight of land, your need to find channel markers in reduced visibility, and so on. At the very least, you should own a handheld GPS system so that you will know your position and course over the ground.

## Tip 2.12  Don't run foul of the FCC

There was a time when it was illegal to operate a radar, VHF radio, handheld VHF radio, single-sideband radio, or EPIRB (Emergency Position-Indicating Radio Beacon) without a license from the Federal Communications Commission (FCC). This rule has changed, however, and licenses are no longer necessary unless your vessel is in commercial use, is traveling in international waters, or will be visiting foreign ports. But, stay tuned to your chandlers, local yacht clubs, and boating publications. The rule could change again. (We discuss FCC licenses in more detail in Tip 4.3 and in Chapter 10, "Miscellany.")

## Tip 2.13  Know your depths

Charts are marked in depths at low water conditions (either mean low tide, mean lower low water, or lowest normal tide according to the area) to indicate the most shallow conditions. They are marked in either feet, meters, or fathoms according to the geographical region and the date the chart was produced. (Charts produced after 1994 are in meters or fathoms.)

Bridges are marked showing the clearance at high tide (so you can be aware of the minimum clearance). Small-scale charts, which show a large area in small detail, typically describe coastal or open ocean areas and because of the extreme depths, show those readings in fathoms (6 feet equal 1 fathom).

Large-scale charts show a small area in great detail. The basis of depth measurement, whether meters, feet, or fathoms, is clearly stated on all charts.

# Chapter 3

# DOCKING

There is something unique about docking. It is a time of connection and resolve, a homecoming, a moment of truth and (hopefully) grace, and often the most critical step in your voyage. More than any other phase of boat handling, it is the time that can try your patience. While docking may be the last part of your voyage, it shouldn't be the last thing you think about. Planning ahead will eliminate oversights and slip-ups and will keep you from marring a good time on the water or the side of your boat.

## Tip 3.1 Have your lines ready

I've often seen boats pulling up to a dock or slip with crew poised to hop off, and no mooring lines ready. What happens next is anyone's guess. Just as often, I've seen crew jump from the deck of a docking vessel, holding a line secured to nothing. Then they have to reach back to secure the line (if they can), while trying to hold the boat with a free hand; or they have to wait until another crewmember can come forward to toss them a line that is secured to the vessel. All this takes time, and every second that passes creates more opportunity for trouble.

There's too much at stake in docking for these preparations to be an afterthought. If there is any kind of current, if there are neighboring vessels, if there is a strong wind blowing, the incoming vessel can easily end up somewhere it's not supposed to be. That can result in damage to the vessel and other boats, and even in injury to a crewmember.

The crew on this boat is ready to depart from amidships (the point of widest beam) with both lines in hand, but he will have to let one go when he decides which one to tie first. With two crew handy, each should have a line and be ready to disembark.

When you come up to the dock, have your line(s) ready, with one end secured to the boat and the remainder of the line led outside the railings. The crew should leave the boat, holding the line(s), the moment it stops— not before it has slowed to a safe speed, and not after the boat has begun to drift away from the dock. Crew should depart from the point of maximum beam (the widest part of the boat), not the bow (front) even though it seems as if the bow will be the first part of the vessel to arrive (see Tip 3.10).

Take care that lines do not fall in the water and get fouled by the turning prop. (My forward dock lines reach from the bow cleats to a point three feet short of the prop, in case they ever do hit the water.)

On small, easily maneuvered boats where the crew is usually seated at dock level, boathooks can be used to secure the vessel before the crew steps onto the dock. Boathooks provide extended reach and should be used to grab the dock cleats, pull the boat up to the dock, and hold it steady as the crew departs.

In a well-managed docking and in the absence of severe currents or winds, there is always plenty of time. Take it.

A dockline flaked over the rail in advance ensures that it will pay out efficiently when the vessel arrives at the dock. Ready it at the last minute and be sure it is carefully hung, so it doesn't slip overboard into the turning prop.

## Tip 3.2  Watch the current and wind

In all but the quietest inland water areas, you need to take currents into account whenever you're docking or picking up a mooring. Where do these currents come from? Tidal changes, river flow, the wakes of passing boats, even the wind working on the water. They can be almost imperceptible, or they can be as potent as the 4- and 5-knot currents found in the San Francisco Bay area.

Keep an eye on the currents as you enter your docking point. The flow of water will have a lot to do with your direction, speed of approach, and the side of the dock you want to make fast to.

Mild or strong, currents cause water to work against the hull of your boat. The effect can create uncontrollable and hazardous variables in your direction of travel as your vessel nears the dock, mooring, or marina entrance. The hazard is compounded if currents catch you unaware.

How do you protect yourself? First, check your tide tables so you know what to expect at the time you'll be docking. Then study the water itself as you approach your destination. What is the direction of flow around buoys and pilings? If there is floating debris, in what direction and how fast is it moving?

Boink! This boat was not tied properly to accommodate a shift in current while at the guest dock. A properly positioned springline would save some gelcoat.

If you are coming up to a dock or mooring (as opposed to a slip where you do not have a choice), judge whether wind or current is exerting the more powerful influence on your boat as you begin to maneuver. If it is the wind, try to dock into the wind, with the wind blowing from ahead. In a crosswind, know whether it will blow you to or from the dock or mooring as you make contact. Take a quick look at sailboat mastheads in your marina. Most, if not all, of them carry wind direction indicators up there.

If the current is the stronger influence, make adjustments for your approach so that you neither slam into nor get carried away from the dock as you near the contact point. In many cases, you may not have a choice, but working the wind and current into your plans will make for a safer, cleaner, smoother contact with the dock. Does the dock have a center cleat? If so, take advantage of it by readying a line from your own center cleat, from the base of a stanchion, or from the base of your shrouds. When led perpendicularly to the dock's center cleat, this breastline is a great way to get the boat settled close to the dock, giving you some time to make the fore and aft lines secure. (This is also a great way to handle the docking process when singlehanding.)

If you remain alert and observant of the conditions around you, docking or picking up a mooring will present no unexpected surprises.

## Tip 3.3  Keep an extra fender handy

In crowded anchorages, you never know when you might find yourself drifting toward another boat (or vice versa). Fenders should be in place *before* you prepare to dock, not after. It is also wise to place a spare fender close at hand so that you will be prepared to fend off any contact with another vessel by lowering the fender between you and your new neighbor. Believe me, that's much safer than you or your crew trying to stave off a collision by using muscle power and body parts.

## Tip 3.4  Practice keeping way on

Sailboats approaching a dock need to be moving through the water to maintain steerage. Twin-engined powerboats have the advantage of being able to work one engine against the other, for close-in maneuverability. But no matter what kind of boat you're in, there comes a point when slowing down too much leaves you without sufficient steerage to dock.

The best place to find that point, for your boat, is away from the dock. Go to some place where you have plenty of room, and practice coming up to a floating fender or an isolated mooring. Keep doing it until you have a feel for the minimum speed at which you can approach a dock and still maintain control of the vessel. (If that floating fender has a line attached, be careful you don't snag it in your prop.)

## Tip 3.5  Let reverse thrust be your brake

In docking a boat, the equivalent of an airplane pilot's three-point landing is to enter the slip, just touch the fenders against the finger float, and ease to a graceful stop without anyone even thinking your bow might hit the main dock or dock box.

If you're tying up to a mooring (see Tip 5.21), you have more latitude, but the idea is the same. You want to come up to your mark smartly, and stop just as smartly.

To do this well takes practice. As in Tip 3.4, you need to know how to maintain steerage until you are alongside the finger slip. Now let's focus on the "graceful stop" technique.

As you come alongside the dock, the transmission should be in neutral with the engine throttled down. Then slip the shift lever into reverse. Allow enough time for the drive system to engage and for the propeller to begin turning in reverse, then apply engine power smoothly to stop your vessel.

Here's an amplified review, going back to the approach we talked about in Tip 3.4.

- Approach the dock or mooring with enough forward momentum to give you steerage. (For most sailboats, this is a speed between 1.5 and 2 knots. Powerboats have better maneuverability than sailboats have at slow speeds but are more easily affected by strong winds due to their high topsides and cabin profiles.)

- When you begin to align the vessel with the dock, and you feel you no longer need forward thrust, bring the engine down to idle. Ease the shift control to neutral.

- When you are about halfway into your destination, shift the engine to reverse. Allow time for the system to engage and for the prop to begin turning in reverse (typically, about three to four seconds). Then apply power as needed to stop the boat.

- As soon as all forward momentum ceases, drop the throttle control to idle and immediately shift into neutral.

   (Always avoid shifting from forward to reverse, without first allowing the engine to slow down to an idle, otherwise you can cause serious damage to the transmission or the propeller shaft and drivetrain.)

- Don't kill the engine yet. Keep it on until you know that all dock lines have been made fast. You may need power in a hurry if a line fails, or if the wind or current moves you out of position before your vessel is secured.

## Tip 3.6  Learn the dynamics of running a sailboat in reverse under power

Most sailboats don't go astern well under power, though there are exceptions. On a boat with a large, deep, spade rudder, no skeg (a downward extension of the hull that supports the rudder's leading edge on some boats), and a prop set low in the water, backward steerage is merely a matter of steering and hanging on tightly to the tiller or wheel. (Caution: The uncentered pivot point on most spade rudders makes it a challenge to keep hold of the tiller when going astern.)

But the majority of production sailboats have little or no steerage while going astern (in reverse) under power. Most boats, in fact, tend to veer to port or to starboard when going astern. The reason is twofold: the wash around the propeller and the wash past the rudder ("prop wash").

When a boat is going astern, if the prop is turning clockwise (looking from the stern) it tends to force the stern to starboard. If the prop is turning counterclockwise (as it most commonly is) it tends to force the stern to port. This is because the deeper water encountered by the prop blades at the bottom of their swing offers more resistance than the water at the top of the revolution. Water nearer the surface is less dense, and can easily rise and splash about the hull. Thus, as the boat goes astern in reverse gear, each of the prop's blades gets a better "bite" toward the bottom of its turn.

The net effect is that the prop tends to "paddle-wheel," working sideways while it is also working astern. The vessel tends to wander off in one direction or another, according to the rotation of the prop, instead of going straight backward.

Why doesn't this happen when the boat is going forward? Well, it does. But when the boat is going forward, the rudder acts like feathers on an arrow (following behind the keel, which is positioned ahead of the prop and rudder), and this keeps the boat headed in a straight line and overcomes any sideways tendency from the prop. Additionally, because the prop is forward of the rudder on inboard drive systems, the thrust of water from the prop streams against the face of the rudder to effect better steerage. When you go astern, the rudder does not have this steering advantage; at slow speed in reverse, it is of little use.

So, what can you do to wring some backward steerage out of this less-than-ideal setup? The trick is to use your reverse gear in short bursts of power, and then immediately throttle down and shift to neutral. As you coast backward with the engine in neutral, you will find you have some (if not exactly eye-popping) steerage with the rudder.

If your boat has a tiller rather than a wheel, use care when backing. Hard turns when backing at moderately fast speeds can generate severe stress loads for the tiller, especially if the rudderpost connects at the leading edge of the rudder. Even at moderate speed, the tiller could swing violently to one side and personal injury could occur.

Whether wheel or tiller, don't allow either to go free while going astern, causing your rudder to slam against the stops. It's not the best thing you can do to the steering assembly.

## Tip 3.7  Learn the dynamics of running a powerboat in reverse

Powerboats with stern drives and outboards are quite easy to steer in reverse. There usually is little need to work one engine against the other for better control since the prop's energy can be turned in the desired direction. However, single fixed-prop powerboats with conventional rudders usually go astern rather poorly. As with many sailboats, their steerage in reverse is a problem (see Tip 3.6).

Likewise, twin fixed-prop powerboats with conventional rudders typically have poor steerage going astern if the rudders are all that are used to aid the turn. But here's where the art of using the engine controls comes in: By adding or decreasing power to either engine, or working one in reverse while the other is working forward, you can exercise reasonably precise control in backing the vessel.

For example, if you apply forward power at idle speed to the starboard engine while you run the port engine in reverse with modest power, the vessel will go astern to starboard.

This skill requires practice, so take a cue from Tip 3.4 and work on your opposing-engines technique away from the dock until you feel you've mastered it.

## Tip 3.8 Don't try to tie a moving vessel

On any given day at any marina, you're apt to see a crewmember hop off a boat just as it is pulling into a slip, and secure the dockline(s) before the vessel has come to a full stop. This may seem like a step-lively, sailorly thing to do, but it's a bad idea. Using a line or lines to stop a moving boat can endanger the boat, the line, the cleats, the dock, the passengers, the working crew, or all of the above.

As the vessel arrives at the dock, the crew disembarks from amidships.

One wrap is taken around a mooring cleat to help slow the vessel.

Once the vessel has stopped, the line can be made secure.

Sail and powerboats must be eased to a stop. Yes, lines should be run around a dock cleat as the vessel is docking, but they should *never* be secured in figure-eights or other wraps until the boat is sitting still. One fast turn around the cleat is all that is needed. Then the crew can slip the line in or out as required, to gently brake any forward movement.

If dock lines are secured before the boat has stopped:

- The boat may come to an abrupt halt, throwing passengers forward with the risk of injury.

- Deck cleats and dock cleats can be severely strained. Often this is how cleats get torn from their mounts.

- Dock lines, especially undersized ones, can snap, leaving the vessel moving forward with nothing to stop it.

- The bow, if made fast (secured) prematurely, may pitch in toward the dock, causing the stern to swing out. That means the crew in the stern can't hand off the stern line, but instead must heave it. If the throw misses, you then have a line in the water near the propeller.

## Tip 3.9  Use cleats, not your hands

In moderate wind and water conditions, it is virtually impossible for an average adult to hold a boat longer than 25 feet to the dock unless the lines are cleated. It's simply too risky to trust someone to hang on to the line. A slip or misstep can leave them hurt, leave neighboring boats damaged, leave a boat gliding away free and unskippered, or worse.

Whether you're arriving or departing, use cleats or rails or posts to secure the lines. When you're getting ready to depart, lines should stay cleated until the skipper gives the command to cast off.

The crew on the dock near the bow should take a turn with the line around a dock cleat. Without cleating the line, the crew's strength is probably no match for the pull of the 38-foot powerboat floating away from the dock.

Let cleats do all the work. One simple turn around the cleat is all that is needed to stop a vessel or hold her in place.

## Tip 3.10 Leave from amidships, not the bow

Crew should never jump down to the dock from the bow (front of the boat). New crewmembers or guests often see this as the quickest way ashore, since the bow is the part of the boat that gets there first. But the quickest way is by no means the safest. The correct point of departure is from the point of maximum beam (the widest and typically the lowest part of the boat, usually just aft of amidships), once the vessel is alongside the dock.

Why? Simple. With the boat alongside the dock, it's an easy step. Moreover, by then the skipper should have slowed the boat sufficiently for the crew to step onto the dock, walk forward, and run the bow line around a cleat before the bow arrives. (Naturally, this means your bow lines must be long enough to reach from the bow to the point of greatest beam, so your crew can disembark with a line in hand.)

Leaping from the bow may be more picturesque, but it's just not prudent. (Exception: if you are on a sailboat with no auxiliary power, luffing up to a dock bow-first may be your typical method of arrival. When approaching a dock or float head on [at right angles to it], departing from the bow is perfectly acceptable. Make every effort to cushion the impact between vessel and dock. Watch your footing. Leave with line in hand.) On smaller, lighter vessels, it may also kick the bow away from the dock, complicating the approach.

This crew is ready with the line, but they are standing in the wrong place. Even though the bow reaches the dock first, the crew should be ready to leave from amidships.

## Tip 3.11  Learn the right way to make fast

The cleat-hitch knot, which goes around the cleat in the shape of a figure eight, is the most effective way to secure a line to a cleat. Optimally, to be sure the lines do not slip free, you can twist each loop (after the first full turn) into a half-hitch so that the eye of the loop locks the line in place.

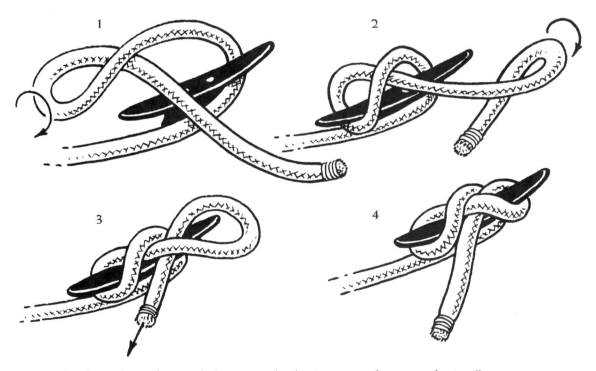

Attaching a line in figure-eight loops around a cleat is not enough to assure that it will not come free. The locking-cleat-hitch provides the best security: 1. Bring the line around the cleat. 2. Twist the line so that each layer is locked in place by the over-wrap. A minimum of two locks is required.

I prefer a minimum of two locking turns around the cleat although the usual recommendation is one. Pull the lines snug to remove any slack. Extra line can be wrapped around the cleat or coiled neatly on deck.

## Tip 3.12 Springlines let you and your boat sleep well

Lines leading perpendicularly from the boat to the dock do not prevent the boat from surging forward or backward (see illustration on page 80). Springlines ensure that the vessel stays in place while attached to the dock, and they're very helpful when you're rafting up (see Tip 5.22 for helpful hints on rafting up to other boats).

Springlines also prove useful in close quarters when you have to turn a large boat at an angle when leaving a slip or dock. For example, if you remove the other dock lines and leave the forward springline in place, the vessel will turn toward the dock when a little forward power is applied. The spring is then released and the crew quickly comes aboard, checking that lines are out of the water and clear of the prop.

## Tip 3.13 Master tying the bowline

Splicing lines together, tying efficient knots, and properly whipping the freshly cut ends of lines are useful talents for boatowners, and entire books are devoted to the marlinspike art of knots and lines. "Efficient" is the key word here. While many knots are fun to tie and look great, in day-to-day boating, most have minimal functionality.

One knot stands out as the king of knotting; I speak of the bowline, of course. Unlike some other knots, the bowline will never jam. No matter how much load is placed upon it, it can be "unlocked" easily when the time comes to untie it.

The illustrations on the next page show how to tie this useful knot in just a few quick twists.

(You may have noticed that I do not use the word "rope." In nautical terms, rope is what we call that stuff when it is in a spool. Once it is cut to workable lengths, it is called "line.")

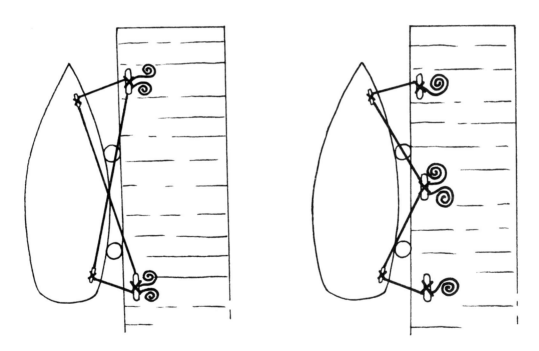

In addition to securing the boat directly to the dock, springlines prevent forward and backward movement. Run the lines from the boat's forward cleats to the dock's after cleats, and so on, or use a center cleat if one is available.

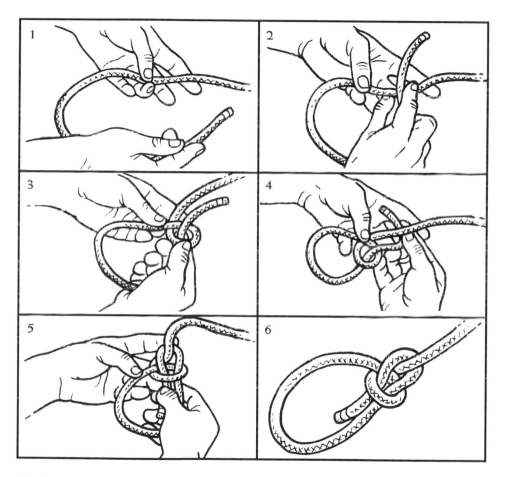

The bowline knot is a boater's best friend. It has tremendous holding power, and can be easily untied no matter how much load is placed on the line. Here's a quick and easy way to tie one: **1**. Take the free end of the loop and place it over the line. **2**. Place your thumb under the intersection of the two lines and twist both lines one half-turn (**3**) until the free end pops out of the loop you just made (by twisting). **4**. Bring the free end behind the line and back (**5**) into the loop. **6**. Pull it snug.

## Chapter 4

# USING YOUR RADIO

My wife was not pleased when I arrived home. The wedding I missed while sailing in the fog was an important and unrepeatable event. I had not called her—I couldn't. I had known where I was, and that Stu and I were safe, but she hadn't. If we'd run into trouble, no one would have known. Nor would we have been able to call the yacht club or any nearby vessel to come to our aid. Although we were only inches from the dock, we were totally out of reach.

We may imagine ourselves as Eric the Red or Christopher Columbus when we're on the water, but they weren't out of touch by choice. Everyone who goes on the water should have communication tools and know how to use them. In this day and age, even with cellular phones commonplace, there is still no substitute for carrying, and knowing how to use, vessel-to-vessel or vessel-to-shore radio communications.

## Tip 4.1  Be certain your radio works

A VHF radio gives you a direct link to the Coast Guard, to other vessels, and to local authorities. In an emergency, it's the most important piece of equipment you have on board. Before you leave the dock, make sure it is working perfectly. You can call another vessel on Channel 16 (see Tip 4.2) for a radio check.

The procedure is to listen to a working channel (68, 69, 71, 72) until you hear two vessels passing traffic (talking), and then, immediately after they've finished and have returned to Channel 16, call one of them *by name* on Channel 16. After making contact this way, go to a working channel and ask for a radio check.

A typical call would go something like this: *"Raven. Raven.* This is the vessel *Bluebird."* If your radio works and if you are heard by another skipper, you should get a quick acknowledgment.

If the *Raven* responds, you would then transmit *"Raven,* this is *Bluebird,* please switch and answer on Channel six eight, over."* You should get a response something like *"Bluebird,* this is *Raven* switching to six eight."* You then switch your radio to Channel 68, make your call again, and ask about the quality of your transmission.

If you don't get a response to your first broadcast to *Raven,* check to see that the radio's squelch control (see Tip 4.4) is turned all the way down—to the point that you can hear background noise—and that the volume control is turned all the way up. Then try another radio check.

If you still get no response, something may be wrong with your radio. Have someone competent look it over, and don't get under way until it is fully operational. It is your only connection to shore.

Many skippers quickly respond with an automatic "radio check loud and clear." However, don't deliver that message if the transmission you heard was not both "loud" and "clear."

For example, you might respond: *"Bluebird, Bluebird,* radio check loud and clear." Or you might say it was "moderate to broken," "poor," "muffled," "weak," and so on. Also remember to give your location. That's important because it establishes a distance between the two boats. If the other boat is 40 miles away, a respectable distance for a 25-watt VHF radio, the skipper may very well be satisfied that you heard him at all, never mind loud and clear.

You may have heard that the Coast Guard provides radio-check services. Not true. Acknowledging radio-check requests is a courtesy among fellow skippers, so be quick to return the favor whenever you have a chance.

## Tip 4.2  Know how to use your radio

Although your radio operates over a wide band of channels, the basic listening channel is Channel 16—officially set aside for safety, hailing, and distress purposes only.

Use it to call another vessel, or call for help in an emergency. You should not use Channel 16 for any other continuous communication, however. There are other channels set aside for this purpose.

For example, if you use Channel 16 to call the Coast Guard for assistance, they will usually ask you to switch to Channel 22A or Channel 9. (The request is apt to be phrased: "Switch to Channel two-two alpha," or "Switch and answer two-two alpha." "Two-two alpha" [22A] is the same as Channel 22 on most VHF radios used in the U.S. even if it doesn't have an "A" after it.)

In addition to Channel 16, Channel 9 is now officially designated for "boater calling" both commercial and noncommercial.

Once you reach a vessel on Channel 16 or Channel 9, radio etiquette and FCC regulations require you immediately to suggest changing to another frequency or "working channel" so that Channel 16 (the hailing and distress channel) and Channel 9 (the boater calling channel) remain clear and available at all times. The accompanying charts give you a channel-by-channel breakdown of your options, but here's a quick overview:

Channel 16 is for general hailing and distress calls only. Monitor it while you're under way. If someone calls you and wants to chat, advise them that you both should switch to a different channel.

Channels 12 and 22A are used by the Coast Guard for information broadcasts and communication.

Channels 6 and 9 are open to both commercial and noncommercial vessels, with Channel 6 reserved for purposes of intership safety.

Channels 68, 69, 71, 72, and 78A are set aside for noncommercial vessels; and of that group, Channels 69, 71, and 78A may be used by marinas, yacht clubs, or other organizations that provide services and supplies to noncommercial vessels.

Channels 65A, 66A, 73, 74, and 77 are limited to port operations radio traffic. It's only appropriate to use these channels when you are in or near a port; in locks; or in waterways—and communication must pertain to the movement of vessels or persons.

Channels 24–28 and 84–88 are used by marine operators, though only two or three are active in any given area. For example, in and around San Francisco Bay, the marine operator answers on Channels 26, 84, and 87. (Many skippers try to call marine operators on Channel 16. Since marine operators do not monitor this channel, there will be no response. Other boaters in the area will usually advise you of the local marine operator channels.)

## VHF RADIO CHANNELS LISTED BY CHANNEL

| | |
|---|---|
| 06 | Intership communications/commercial and noncommercial/safety only |
| 07A | Intership communications/commercial only |
| 08 | Intership communications/commercial only |
| 09 | Boater calling, commercial and noncommercial |
| 12 | Port operations/nondistress, marine information broadcasts |
| 13 | Navigational information/Vessel Traffic Service |
| 16 | All vessels/distress, safety, and hailing/*monitor this channel while under way* |
| 22A | Coast Guard/main communications and announcements |
| 24 to 28 | Marine operator |
| 65A and 66A | Port operations |
| 67 | Intership communications/commercial |
| 68 | Intership communications/noncommercial |
| 69 | Intership communications/noncommercial/marine service providers |
| 70 | Future DSC (see Tip 10.3)/noncommercial |
| 71 | Intership communications/noncommercial/marine service providers |
| 72 | Intership communications/noncommercial |
| 73 and 74 | Port operations/communications about waterway traffic |
| 77 | Port operations/intership only |
| 78A | Intership communications/noncommercial/marine service providers |
| 80A | Commercial |
| 84 to 87 | Marine operator |
| 88A | Intership communications/commercial only |

## VHF RADIO CHANNELS LISTED BY USAGE

## Tip 4.3  Tune in to the FCC's requirements for a radio station license

Until the enactment of the Telecommunications Act of 1996 (effective February 8, 1996), it was illegal to operate a VHF radio, handheld VHF radio, single-sideband radio, a navigational radar system, or even an Emergency Position-Indicating Radio Beacon (EPIRB) unless you held a valid FCC license for doing so.

The rules have changed.

The new regulation stipulates that relative to radio usage, there are two categories of vessels: "compulsory ships" and "voluntary ships." Compulsory ships include large passenger or cargo ships that travel on the open sea, and passenger ships that travel along the coast. Compulsory ships are compelled by the Telecommunications Act (and by international agreements) to be equipped with a radio station for long-distance or coastal radio communications. Voluntary ships are smaller vessels used for recreation (sailing, diving, fishing, water skiing, and so on). Voluntary ships are not required to have radio stations but may do so voluntarily.

The law goes on to state that ship stations may communicate with other ship stations or coast stations primarily for safety, and secondarily for navigation and operational efficiency.

Although it may seem that the rules have been relaxed a bit, the FCC and Coast Guard have not relaxed their grip on the proper usage of marine radios. Proper channel usage, vessel identification, and radio decorum must still be adhered to.

Don't think that there are too many users for the FCC to keep track of, or that you'll be overlooked in the static. I know of a boater with an expired license, back when licenses were required, who used his outdated call sign on the air. Shortly thereafter, he received a polite letter from the

FCC suggesting that he get up-to-date—or else. They *do* listen, and the usage rules must be followed.

For specifics of the Telecommunications Act of 1996, see chapter 10, "Miscellany."

### Tip 4.4 Master the perfect squelch

Boaters new to VHF radio often are mystified by the squelch adjustment knob, but its use is simple. The squelch is a kind of threshold control for suppressing background noise—noise that is always present, no matter what radio frequency you're on.

The squelch is a noise filter. Turn it until you hear loud background noise, then turn it back just enough to cut out the noise.

With the squelch control turned off its noisiest setting, your receiver isn't very discriminating. It delivers good transmissions, garbled transmissions, and random static (for example, other VHF users who aren't close enough to be heard, but who collectively create "noise"). It's not pretty, and not helpful when you're trying to carry on a conversation.

As the squelch control is turned up, you progressively mask or filter more of the background noise on that frequency. With the noise removed, incoming signals from vessels transmitting within radio range come through with greater clarity. The trick is to learn when to stop. With the squelch turned up too much, you may suppress signals you probably want to hear. Turn it up too little, and you will have a great deal of unwanted noise. (Of course, if a vessel is a half-mile away and is transmitting at a hefty 25 watts, it will break through the squelch regardless. But you won't encounter that very often.)

Learn to turn your squelch knob just to the point where it cuts off the background noise and then back it off slightly (toward adding background noise). Foreground messages will be much easier to follow. Any weaker messages would be too noise-ridden to make out, anyway. If you are cruising on the high seas (where there is very little radio noise), it is wise to leave your squelch fully open (off) so that you can hear distant signals.

## Tip 4.5  Know your transmitter's range

VHF radio signals travel "line-of-sight" pathways. That is, the signals can be disrupted by mountains or islands, and will not normally be received far over the horizon. Don't expect them to go around obstacles.

How far your radio transmissions travel depends on how much power your system packs, measured in watts, and the height and quality of your antenna and antenna wiring. On open water, a 25-watt VHF in good working order has a range of about 30 miles. The effective range is even greater if the transmitting antenna is high off the water; still more if the receiving antenna and system, such as the Coast Guard's, is well-installed, strategically positioned, and of high quality.

When set to 1 watt, which is the legal setting for transmissions on bays and inland waterways, the range of a VHF is about 3 miles. Handheld VHF radios set to 1 watt have somewhat less range than their full-sized relatives, primarily because their antennas are shorter and typically nearer the surface of the water. A handheld 5-watt VHF has a range of about 5 miles. (You can get better performance from any handheld VHF by being sure to hold its antenna straight up and down.)

## Tip 4.6  Speak the language like a native

The FCC has developed radio standards that all boaters, military, commercial, and civilian alike are expected to follow. If you're familiar with CB (Citizens Band) radio jargon, forget it. Phrases such as "Ten-four," "Negative copy," and "What's your 10-20?" are out of place in the marine world. You need to speak the right language to be understood.

While writing this section of *Boating 101*, sitting in a quiet cove on San Francisco Bay, I picked up a signal from a boater calling, "Coast Guard Central, Coast Guard Central." He wasn't getting an answer, even though we have a very responsive and helpful Coast Guard Group in the Bay. After a few minutes, Coast Guard Group San Francisco came on the radio and asked if he was calling them.

The Coast Guard wasn't being stuffy. More than likely, they weren't sure who the vessel was calling. (Fortunately, the vessel wasn't in trouble, nor did the Coast Guard wait very long before responding.)

In some complex bays and waterways, there are several Coast Guard stations, and even more Coast Guard Auxiliary facilities. While a call to "Coast Guard" will eventually bring a response, a quicker answer will probably come from directing your call to the desired station. (Another good reason to listen to the chatter on your VHF radio is to become acquainted with the proper names of your local services.)

Here are some guidelines for communicating effectively on your radio:

1.  Begin each transmission with the name of the vessel you are calling, followed by your vessel's name.

2.  Say "Over" at the end of each transmission, so the receiving party knows you've completed your part of the communication and are expecting a reply.

3. When initiating a call to another vessel, use its name at least twice to ensure they will hear and recognize the call.

4. It is proper procedure to include your FCC call sign in your opening call. (While FCC licenses are no longer required [see Tip 10.2], you should use your call sign if you have one.)

5. Avoid using CB jargon or law-enforcement radio codes. They aren't acceptable for VHF communications.

Taking all this into consideration, here is an example of how a basic communication might go. Let's assume you're the caller, aboard the vessel *Pelican,* and you begin by hailing the Coast Guard on Channel 16:

"Coast Guard Group Jones Island. Coast Guard Group Jones Island. This is *Pelican,* Whiskey Sierra Mike seven seven two two." (Your boat's name is *Pelican;* your call sign is WSM 7722.)

Pause.

If you hear nothing after 15 seconds, try the call again, making sure you are on Channel 16. When the Coast Guard answers, you might hear "Vessel calling. This is Coast Guard Group Jones Island, Channel 16."

This indicates they didn't clearly understand or have time to record your vessel's name and call sign but heard they were being called. In that case, you would repeat your original call to identify yourself. On the other hand, if they did hear you the first time they might answer (some of the "buzz words" are explained in the subsequent paragraph) "*Pelican,* this is Coast Guard Group Jones Island. Switch and answer Channel two two alpha; two two alpha. Over."

They want you to switch to Channel 22A. Acknowledge by saying:

"Coast Guard, this is *Pelican* switching to two two alpha."

Switch your radio to Channel 22A (the same as "22" on most recreational boating VHF radios) and call them back, following the format of your first call: "Coast Guard Group Jones Island, this is *Pelican*, Whiskey Sierra Mike seven seven two two."

The rest of the conversation might go something like this:

"*Pelican*, Coast Guard. Roger, skipper; please state your traffic, over."

"Coast Guard, *Pelican*. There is a large piling floating near Drake's Marina. Over."

"*Pelican*, Coast Guard. Roger, skipper. We will notify the Drake's Marina harbormaster. Over."

"Coast Guard, *Pelican*. Thank you for your help. This is *Pelican* switching back to sixteen."

"*Pelican*, Roger that. Coast Guard, out."

"*Pelican*, out."

You have completed your call. Switch the radio back to Channel 16.

## GLOSSARY OF BASIC VHF TERMS AND PHRASES

*Affirmative.* "Yes."

*Copy? Did you copy that?* or *I did not copy* means "Did you understand?" or "I did not understand."

*Last* or *Your last* refers to the last thing you said, as in the request *Repeat your last.*

*Negative.* "No."

*Nothing heard.* You tried to reach another vessel and they did not respond.

*Out.* "I am ending my communication and am

- getting off this channel or
- discontinuing my conversation with you or
- not continuing to work at the radio right now."

*Over.* Shorthand for "My immediate conversation is finished. Over to you."

*Roger.* "Okay." More specifically, *Roger that* means "I understand it" or "I agree with you."

*Say again your last.* "Would you repeat that, please?"

*Switch and answer two two alpha.* "Change the channel on your radio to 22A and respond."

*Stand by.* "Wait a moment, until I respond."

*State your traffic.* "Speak up. Pass your message."

*Traffic.* Radio communications, the dialogue or message itself.

95

## THE PHONETIC CODE

When spelling a name or giving a call sign, letters are difficult to differentiate clearly over the air. The proper thing to do is to use words beginning with the desired letter. Here are the approved standard words of the International Phonetic Code. (However, in a pinch, any word will do in order to make yourself understood. For example, you could substitute "apple" for "alpha." It may not be stylish, but it will be clear.)

| | |
|---|---|
| Alpha | November |
| Bravo | Oscar |
| Charlie | Papa |
| Delta | Quebec |
| Echo | Romeo |
| Foxtrot | Sierra |
| Golf | Tango |
| Hotel | Uniform |
| India | Victor |
| Juliet | Whiskey |
| Kilo | Xray |
| Lima | Yankee |
| Mike | Zulu |

## Tip 4.7  Get acquainted with the marine operator

Most coastal and major inland water regions are served by a marine phone service, accessible on your VHF radio and linking you directly to the local telephone system. These marine radio services normally operate over two or three frequencies. If neighboring areas are served by separate marine radio networks, the stations are assigned different channels in order to avoid confusion and possible interference.

For example, the San Francisco marine operator works on VHF Channels 26, 84, and 87. The Stockton marine operator (based about 60 miles east of San Francisco) works on Channels 25, 86, and 88.

If a marine operator has a call for you, you will get an alert call on Channel 16. The call usually is preceded by a tone designed to get your attention. A typical call might begin like this: Beep! "Pelican, Pelican. This is the Stockton marine operator calling the vessel Pelican. Call sign Whiskey Sierra Mike seven seven two two [if the person calling you knows your call sign]. Owner, Bob Jones. Please contact Stockton marine operator on Channels 25, 86, or 88. We have traffic for you. Stockton marine operator out."

If you were Bob Jones or one of the crew on the Pelican, you would switch to one of those channels, first making sure no one else was communicating on it, and you would reply "Stockton marine operator, Stockton marine operator, this is Pelican, Whiskey Sierra Mike seven seven two two. You have traffic for us."

The marine operator would respond, verify that you were in fact Bob Jones aboard the Pelican, and connect you with your caller. Later, after your caller hangs up, you would hail the marine operator on the same channel and say you had completed your "traffic." The channel is then available for someone else.

Your callers need to be prepared for single-channel radio communication, since they will be using a telephone, but you'll be on your VHF and therefore unable to talk and listen at the same time. Explain this ahead of time to your callers so you won't be talking over one another. Your caller (on land) can connect with the marine operator by calling the local telephone operator and asking for the connection. Your caller will be asked for your name, your vessel's name, the body of water or general area you are boating in, and your state registration numbers or document number.

Can you make outgoing calls through the marine operator on your VHF radio? Certainly. But keep in mind that you're using public VHF radio channels, and it's not wise to broadcast your credit-card number. I made that mistake once during a coastal trip from Newport Beach to San Francisco and got a $4,500 surprise phone bill. Fortunately for me, the security department at the phone company was able to track down the caller (of course, the phone company had a record of every number called) who had copied and used my card number, and recovered the money due.

I was lucky that time. Charge calls to your home number—it costs only a few dollars and it's safer.

For commercial ship-to-shore radio telephoning, Maritel, the largest marine operator, has for years encrypted the ship-to-shore portion of the transmission. No one hears you except the marine operator and the person you're calling, so it is perfectly safe to give credit-card numbers.

Considering the widespread use and efficiencies of cellular phones, it may be more efficient to use cellular phones for calls to on-land facilities (nonmarine related) when you are in close proximity to land.

## Tip 4.8 Know the emergency radio rules

Aside from the general comfort of having a VHF aboard, the greatest advantage comes when the radio is needed to communicate an important general-purpose or emergency message. These calls are also intended for the general audience; rather than being sent to one particular station, they are transmitted for any vessel monitoring the radio. There are three stages of alert that are repeated three times prior to the message:

**Securite** (pronounced "say-cure-ee-TAY") precedes any navigational or weather warning of importance to all boaters.

**Pan-Pan** (pronounced "pahn-pahn") precedes a very urgent message concerning the safety of the ship or some person on board. It does not imply that the vessel herself is in *immediate* danger. This message may request the assistance of boaters in the area.

**Mayday** is an alert of the highest urgency and should be used only when the vessel or a crewmember are in immediate and serious danger. This message mandates the assistance of any boaters in the area. An example of an urgent message transmission would be: "Pan-Pan, Pan-Pan, Pan-Pan, this is the vessel *Happy Days*. We have one person in the water near Buoy 4 at the north side of the estuary. Repeat. One person in the water near Buoy 4. Requesting assistance. *Happy Days* standing by."

The phrase "standing by" suggests that you are awaiting a response. Once you establish communication with another vessel or with the Coast Guard, your dialogue should continue as described in Tip 4.6.

A few rules of order:

● The call is transmitted as a general alarm to any station.

● Be as specific as you can about your location. If you are on a small lake and there is only one "Buoy 4," that is sufficient, but on the approach to the East River coming from Long Island Sound, you need to describe your precise location. Be ready with latitude and longitude data (assuming that your loran or GPS is on and you have been monitoring it). Giving a detailed statement of your location will cut valuable time off the search-and-rescue mission.

● Never send a message for other than its priority level. For example, if you are out of fuel and drifting, all crew is safe and the vessel is not in immediate danger, you should only send a "Securite" alert, never a "Pan-Pan" or a "Mayday" alert. Elevate the alert message only when and if the need arises.

● Take the time to train your family and regular crew. Many a safety call has been placed and aided by youngsters who knew how to handle themselves on the radio. Unfortunately, many prank Mayday calls often come from children, or adults acting like children, who do not realize the serious nature of these announcements.

## IF YOU HEAR A CALL . . .

● If an emergency call is in progress and you are not part of the response or assistance effort, *do not transmit on that frequency until the emergency status has been eliminated and communication about it ceases.*

● If you are within range of assistance, you should make every effort to come to the aid of the vessel in distress, to the extent that it does not put you, your crew, or your vessel in jeopardy.

IF YOU HAVE AN EMERGENCY . . .

- Stay calm. Those coming to your aid will need to have clear, concise communication with you.

- Don't shout into the microphone (there's a natural tendency to shout when calling for emergency assistance). Shouting will only result in your being asked to repeat your last transmission, eating up valuable time. Relax. State your message and requirements clearly.

- Be patient. Aid can only come as fast as it can.

- Don't get frustrated. If you communicate with the Coast Guard, they will ask you questions like: "What is the name of your vessel?" "How many people are on board?" "What are your state registration numbers?" and so on. They will probably advise you to have everyone put on a life preserver, and it may appear that they are not being responsive to your immediate needs.

There are several issues here:

1. When you are on the water, the Coast Guard is your best friend. If you need help, they will help you and they know how.

2. They will not send out the First Battalion unless they know who you are, where you are, and what your problem is.

3. While they are preparing to help you, they want to be sure you and your crew remain safe and calm.

4. One aspect of their dialogue is to get you relaxed and feeling secure that you are communicating with them.

### Tip 4.9  Avoid the "Hey you" trap

My favorite transmissions sound like this: "Hey you! Slow down. This is a narrow channel!" Often, these bizarre calls from nowhere to no place are repeated and elevated in intensity, occasionally growing to "Hey—I'm talking to *you!*"

Who is *you?* Where is the caller?

Identify the vessel in question by type, direction, and location. Then add a description of your vessel. You are more apt to get an acknowledgment if your transmission sounds something like this: "This is the vessel *Seagull* to the red-and-white tanker proceeding westward, two miles south of Osborne Light. I am the white cabin cruiser one mile southeast of you, heading north. Over."

Now that you have provided your name (and you may wish to include your call sign), your call should evoke a response along with the name and call sign of the approaching vessel.

Your communications must be from a known station to a known station. If you don't have a vessel's name or call sign, "Hey you" could be any one of a thousand boats within radio range.

If you have a hand-bearing compass, or binoculars with an internal compass, you can provide your exact bearing from the vessel, and its bearing to you. The more accurate your fix, the better.

In foggy conditions, if you are equipped with radar, your call would be similar except that you would not know the type or color of the other vessel, nor would it be able to recognize any of the physical characteristics of your boat. However, the positional information and basic communication would be much like your visual-contact call. For example, you might say: "This is the vessel *Seagull,* Whiskey Sierra Lima five five two eight, to the vessel proceeding westward at approximately thirty-six degrees, fifteen minutes north latitude, one-hundred-eighteen degrees thirty-six minutes west longitude. I am one mile southeast of you, heading north. Do you copy? Over."

Effective and clear dialogue is critical to a safe passage.

# Chapter 5

# ANCHORING

There isn't a part of boating I don't love. Maintenance, brightwork, setting sail, motoring, currents, calm, rain, wind, sea gulls, snacks, and good friends are but a few of the countless pleasures on my list. But the part of it I love the most is riding to an anchor in a quiet cove, contemplating the sun as it drops into the sea. It heralds the culmination of a day on the water, and it is a time when I begin thinking about a warm meal and making preparations to sleep soundly, secure in the knowledge that the anchor I set will hold my position through the night.

## Tip 5.1 Select the right anchor

Anchors come in five basic types. You probably will use only one or two of them, but it is important to be acquainted with the others.

*Mushroom anchors.* The mushroom is a small, simple, round-bottomed weight used mainly to secure small rowboats and dinghies when there is little wind or current. Since this anchor merely sits on the bottom and doesn't bite into anything (unless it gets snarled in seabed growth), it shouldn't be used for boats more than 10 feet long.

(Note: Large mushroom anchors are used for permanent moorings. They are designed to sink into mud over a period of time and create enormous suction if an upward pull is applied.)

*Fisherman* or *hook anchors.* Mention the word "anchor," and this is the image that comes to most people's minds: the classic double-pointed device with a single cross-arm. Fisherman anchors were one of the earliest anchor designs, and over the centuries they have appeared in many variations. They bite well into the seabed, and require a lot of power to bring them up (since they are also very heavy). The flukes also are prone to snagging on rocks (which is what you want them to do on rocky bottoms), and just about anything else they get close to.

*CQR* (for *se-cu-re*) and *Bruce anchors.* These anchor designs are very similar, except that the CQR has a pivoting, pointed-tip plow, while the Bruce has a fixed, round-ended plow. Both are very good in sand and mud and will—as will any anchor—latch onto tall coral or rock (they are not satisfactory on smooth and flat coral, or rock bottoms like some in the Caribbean). They are moderately successful in grass. CQR and Bruce anchors need to be comparatively heavy so they will take a firm bite when dragged along the sea floor. Either type has good holding power and makes a fine No. 1 anchor.

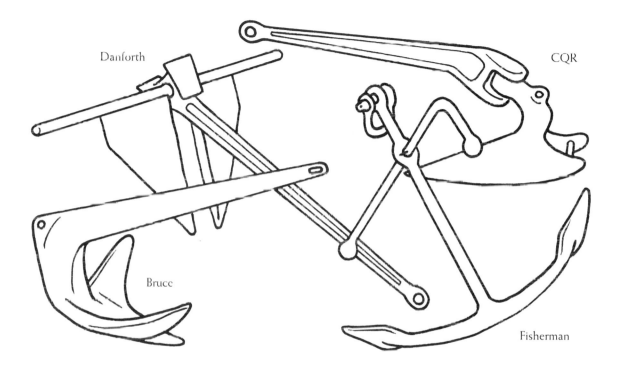

Danforth

CQR

Bruce

Fisherman

Anchors· The **Danforth** is probably the most popular anchor for powerboats and sailboats under 50 feet. It has good holding qualities in grass, sand, and mud but limited or no holding power in rock and clay bottoms. A major advantage is the welded construction and comparatively light weight. **CQR** anchors are heavier, size-for-size, than Danforths and have excellent holding qualities in sand and mud. They are two-piece steel forgings with a swiveling crown. The cast high-tensile steel, one-piece **Bruce** anchor holds well in rocky, sandy, and muddy bottoms, but generally has limited holding power in grass. **Fisherman** anchors are very popular on the East Coast and provide great holding power in most environments, especially on grassy and rocky bottoms.

*Danforth.* Danforth-type anchors usually are fabricated with a stamped-and-welded aluminum or galvanized steel pivoting head, with two sharply pointed blades. They generally are lightweight, bite well in sand and mud, and are good in grass. The Danforth also will hold well in coral or rock, sometimes to the extent that the points can get slightly sprung apart and jammed—which may result in a jump overboard to free the anchor. This anchor has great holding power. Its light weight and low profile make it an ideal No. 2 (stern or bow) anchor that will spend most of its time stowed in a lazarette or anchor locker, ready for emergencies.

Which kind of anchor is best for your boat? Here are some factors to consider before getting out your checkbook:

- Is the anchor's weight appropriate for your boat's size? And, can you handle and weigh it (haul it in) and its additional, yet necessary, chain?

- What are the sea-bottom conditions in the areas where you normally cruise? Here are some basic guidelines:

**Mud.** Good holding power requires that the anchor be seated deeply into mud. This calls for an anchor with a wide angle between its shank and its flukes (blade portion).

- Sufficient scope (see Tip 5.10) must be provided when setting the anchor to assure that the flukes are allowed to dig in and are not dragged across the mud's surface.

Hard mud or clay can be tricky, and heavier anchors do better. Generally, CQR, Danforth, and Bruce anchors do well in mud.

**Sand.** Most anchor designs, including Danforth, CQR, and Bruce work well in sand as long as sufficient scope is payed out.

**Grass.** Grass can be stubborn because it prevents an anchor from digging into the underlying mud. Danforth and Fisherman designs work well because their flukes are sharply pointed and will tend to part the grass and dig into the bed. Danforth anchors can also snag the grass, giving a false sense of security. In areas of little or no current, the snagged grass could hold the vessel overnight. If there are strong currents or swells, however, a mild jolt could tear the grass out, and the anchor will come free.

**Rocks.** Good holding power in rock depends on exactly where you drop the anchor. The good news is that the anchor might snag perfectly around a rock. The bad news is that you might have to dive to pull it free. (I've labored to free the flukes of a Danforth that were spread around a jagged rock.) Fisherman, Danforth, CQR, and Bruce are all capable performers in rocky areas.

**Shale or smooth rock.** These are the toughest bottoms and you may have to try repeatedly until you find that one crack or grassy spot where your anchor will take a bite. If you are at all in doubt, set another anchor from the bow (see Tip 5.14).

**Mixed or unsure.** Carry a combination of anchors such as a Danforth and a CQR. Favor the heavier one (CQR). (Keep it and your anchor line ready or, better yet, properly mounted on your bowsprit.) If it fails to take hold, change to the Danforth and give it a try.

- What kind of anchor-storage facilities do you have aboard? Will the anchor be stored in a lazarette or an anchor locker where you will need to wrestle it free; or will it fit into anchor chocks at the bowsprit? Heavy canvas bags with fabric handles create excellent storage for an anchor line and chain. Be sure you leave the tail end of the line sticking out of the bag (so you can tie it off before you set the anchor) before you flake (see Tip 5.3) in the rest of the line and chain.

- How much can you afford? Do not skimp here. It is a wise investment to buy a good anchor, properly sized chain, and high-quality nylon anchor line.

Your marine dealer has charts to help you match the correct anchor with the corresponding boat length, type, and weight.

A final word on anchoring. Anchors cause damage to coral and other sea life. In most tropical regions of the world, it is illegal to anchor in coral. Whenever possible, use moorings or other anchorages.

## Tip 5.2  Think of chain as your anchor's partner

To set an anchor properly, and keep it set, you need to have ample chain at the bottom end of the anchor rode (the correct name for the entire anchor line).

The chain serves two crucial functions. First, it provides a strong, wear-proof material as the rode drags along the sea bed, over rocks or coral. Second, it puts weight where it is needed most: between the anchor and the boat.

Why is this extra weight important? Once the anchor is set, and the boat is at rest, the chain's weight will draw the boat in to settle directly above the free portion of the anchor rode (as long as there is no strong current or wind making the vessel pull against the anchor).

When a breeze or a shift of current causes the boat to move back, the lifting of the chain from the sea bed acts as an interim anchor long before the real anchor has to deliver holding power. In moderate current conditions, the pulling energy transmitted towards the anchor may be absorbed just by the chain's being lifted from the seabed without the pull ever reaching the anchor itself.

The weight of the chain also acts as a snubber, moderating shocks between the rode and the deck cleats. Lastly, the weight of the chain usually forces the chain end of the rode to sit at a low angle relative to the anchor. A pull at that angle improves the plowing and digging-in action of the anchor blades.

How much chain do you need? It depends on the size of the boat and, to a lesser extent, on where you will be cruising. Typically, you should have a little more than one boatlength of chain. For example, for boats between 30 feet and 45 feet in length, an ideal length would be 50 feet of chain (not including the nylon line attached to the chain). The more chain you have, the more you can shorten scope (the ratio of the depth of water to the length of the total anchor line, see Tip 5.10, Allow ample scope) but never go below 4 to 1.

## Tip 5.3  Use the right mix of chain and line

Unless you have an oceangoing monster, such as a large cargo vessel, or are involved in long-distance cruising, it is usually impractical to carry all your anchor rode as chain. Weight and space considerations dictate the use of line in combination with chain. But there are other reasons to have line as part of your anchor system.

Incidentally, remember that in marine terms, line is called rope when it's on a spool. As soon as it's cut to working length, it becomes line.

When riding to an anchor in heavy seas or strong currents, the line between the chain and the anchor serves as an excellent shock-absorber. Chain, after all, doesn't stretch. The only risk is that if the strain gets too great (which it rarely does), the line could part. On the other hand, under those conditions if you had an all-chain rode, you could be tearing bollards and cleats from your deck. There is a trade-off.

If you have an all-chain rode, you affix a nylon line on the chain, and ease out 30 feet or so to act as a spring, leaving the chain slack between attachment points. This will reduce the possibility of tearing out deck fittings.

And here's another tip: Use the best-quality anchor line you can buy. Otherwise, you risk losing your anchor, or worse. Nylon is preferred for anchor line, where stretchiness is an advantage. Dacron is preferred for a sailboat's sheets (rigging lines) and halyards, where stretchiness is a disadvantage.

How much anchor rode (the combination of line and chain) do you need? The rule of thumb, for general cruising, is to carry 10 times as much rode as the average depth of the local waters. For example, if you typically cruise in waterways with an average depth of 25 feet, you need at least 250 feet of readily available anchor rode.

(Note that "readily available" are the operative words here. Anchors should always be ready to use at a moment's notice, not just when you're setting anchor for the night.)

Then, to be safe, you should have another few hundred feet of comparable, easily attachable line stored where you can find it quickly. Just in case.

Flake the line and chain into your anchor well or into a box (plastic crates are great). Flaking is the process of putting the line into the storage space by allowing it to fall as it may, coiling one loop over another as it goes in, and—most importantly—not disturbing, twisting, or moving the line (other than pushing it down) once it goes into the box. Flaking ensures that the line will come out as easily as it went in, without snagging.

How much anchor rode should you let out? See Tip 5.10, Allow ample scope.

## Tip 5.4  Wear gloves to protect your hands

Whenever you set or weigh (recover) the anchor, always wear sturdy full-finger gloves. Consider this: When a vessel is backing up at 3 knots, the anchor line is paying out at the rate of 5 feet per second. If you are letting that line out through your hands, it is moving fast enough to give you a severe rope burn, which could put you out of commission for several days. And any safety wires or other debris in the chain or line can cause nasty cuts. Protect yourself by keeping a pair of heavy gloves in your anchor locker, and by wearing them any time you work with the anchor line. Inexpensive hardware-grade heavy cotton gloves work well.

## Tip 5.5  Know how to choose an anchorage

There are two types of anchorages: those you select, and those that select you. (Hint: Always try for the former.) The right anchorage is one with a bottom that won't foul your anchor—a sand or mud bottom, preferably, and one that is free of branches, thick kelp, or other growth. Ideally it should be in a quiet sheltered harbor or cove, away from any prevailing current.

If you are in a popular boating area, the best anchorage will be easy to find because at least one other boat will be anchored there already. The types of boats anchored there will tell you something about the bottom and the depths. Boats clustered together may suggest that other locations in that anchorage are undesirable. If you want peace and quiet away from other boaters, you may get it only at the price of less-than-optimum bottom conditions.

Should you tie up to a shore, rather than anchor off it? Don't be too hasty. Tying up to a tree or shrub may give local bugs a gangplank to your boat. You're likely to have fewer insect problems if you anchor farther out.

If you do tie up to shore, you will need to set an anchor anyway, so that your boat lies perpendicular to the shoreline at all times and isn't free to come ashore. That brings up another question: Should you anchor stern-to, or bow-to? The best option normally is to anchor with your bow to the shore; this keeps your rudder and propellers farther away from any obstacles in the shallow water.

In many countries, it is customary to tie up to a quay or man-made wall, and to do so stern-to. Typically, these walls drop off to deep enough water so that there is no risk to your rudder or propeller.

Take a quick look at your chart. Are there any hazards in the anchorage that will snag you or your anchor? If so, stay clear. Where are the best depths for anchoring? The shallower the water, the less chain and line you will have to weigh when ready to leave. Where are the shallows to stay away from when entering or leaving? Assure that you have clear access. And, what will that area be like at low tide? You don't want to wake up in the morning with your boat stuck in the mud.

Finally, be aware of cable crossings, a common attraction for anchors. Cable crossings are marked on most charts and are usually indicated by signs on both shores immediately above the crossing points. Check the positioning of those signs to be sure you are not anchoring in line with them.

## Tip 5.6  Keep an eye on your neighbors

When anchoring near other boats, there are several things to keep in mind as you pick your spot:

- Check for the anchor rodes of other boats as you enter an anchorage so that your propeller and keel do not find them first. Have a crewmember positioned at the bow to look for lines leading from both the bow and the stern. (Sharp boaters will mark their lines with buoys or floating bottles tied to the rode or anchor but don't assume that these will be in use.) Remind your crewmembers to turn and face you as they shout their discoveries.

- Maintain a safe distance from other boats at all times, while maneuvering and at anchor. You don't want to cut across someone else's anchor line.

- Be sure that your swing—the circle your boat would make if it were to rotate fully around the point where your anchor is set—won't intersect the swing of any other boat. In all but the calmest conditions, your boat and your neighbor's boat will most likely swing the same way. Therefore, it is okay to be in tight quarters for a few hours if you are keeping a constant anchor watch, but don't rely on it for an overnight stay.

- You need to use a stern anchor (thus preventing any swing) if other boats are doing so (see Tip 5.15). If they stay in one place and don't swing, you must, too. (If you feel you need to use a stern anchor even if your neighbors don't, be sure to stay well clear of their swing.) More about this in Tip 5.11.

## Tip 5.7  Agree on hand signals

Weighing (recovering) your anchor is easier if the boat is steered along the course of the rode toward the anchor; a route that is easily seen from the bow and all but invisible from the helm. The crewmember on the bow plays a vital role here and teamwork is key.

Whether you are on a 15-foot boat or a 55-foot boat, it's almost impossible to hear someone at the bow yelling instructions when you're at the stern with the engine roaring in your ear. Maneuvering is a lot easier when you and your crew communicate with clearly understood hand signals, instead of verbal commands.

You can invent your own set of signals, but the most common ones are self-explanatory. Your bow person points straight up to indicate going ahead, points right to indicate a turn to starboard, or points left to indicate a turn to port. The signal for "Stop!" is a closed fist or a fully open hand (a bit easier to recognize at a distance). An arm swung in a circular motion above the head means "power up," whether you're moving astern while setting the anchor, or moving forward while weighing anchor.

On a sailboat, the bow person should kneel so you can clearly see the signals under the sails and rigging. Anyone else assisting forward should be out of the way, not blocking the vision from the helm.

Your call to drop the anchor usually will be heard without difficulty, since you're facing forward and the bow person is far from engine noise. In high winds, however, he or she may have to look back for your hand signal—the familiar thumbs-up.

Whatever signals you choose, work them out in advance. It's well worth the effort, and you and your crew will look like pros while everyone else in the anchorage is watching you. Anchoring is no time for improvisation.

The unspoken word is very powerful. The crew at the bow is directing the helmsman to the anchor's future resting point.

## Tip 5.8  Keep an eye on the currents

If there is a current, head into it as you set your anchor. Otherwise, you stand the chance of being pushed off course and away from your chosen anchoring spot. In addition, you can allow your boat to drift back as you make the anchor line secure. If the current is steady (as it would be in a river), your boat should hang on the anchor, riding to it the same way, and facing in the same direction throughout your stay.

If you're in an area with shifting currents (as in an area affected by tidal changes), then you could be in jeopardy were the boat to swing 180 degrees. Should that occur, the radical change in the direction of pull might tear the anchor free.

If you notice currents changing drastically, find a better spot or, for insurance, lay out a stern anchor (see Tip 5.15) to keep the boat from swinging. If you're still concerned, you may have to take turns with your crew and set up an anchor watch throughout the night. It's better for each of you to lose a little sleep than for all of you to lose the boat.

## Tip 5.9  Think deep thoughts

You may not be able to see the bottom at your anchorage, but you need to know as much as possible about it before dropping anchor. Check your charts for the bottom characteristics and adjust your anchoring strategy accordingly. Bottom conditions for typical anchorage areas, specifically regions close to the shore, are indicated on all major charts.

**Mud** has good holding power, so much so that it sometimes may be very stubborn about releasing your anchor. Tip 5.19 tells you how to deal with stubborn anchors. CQRs are great in mud.

**Grass** can fool you. You may think your anchor has a good bite on the bottom, only to find it is actually snagged in some tall grass. One good pull, and the grass, your anchor, and you can go for a slide. Danforths and CQRs do a good job in grass because their sharp points will usually penetrate the grass and dig into the seabed.

**Sand** (if it is deep, not just a thin layer over rock or coral) holds and releases an anchor well; but in sand you need to stay close to the 7-to-1 scope rule (see Tip 5.10). With the proper scope, Danforths, CQRs and Bruce anchors work well in sand.

**Rock and coral** are another problem altogether. Hooking a rock is a great way to hold your boat, except that if you're using a Danforth anchor and the two points get jammed into the rock, you may have to dive to release it. Moreover, if the boat swings, the anchor could easily fall free of the rock, leaving you with no holding power at all. The same is true for coral except that under a jerking load, coral can break. Anchoring in coral is forbidden in many marine sanctuaries and should be avoided in any event. Destroying coral is not ecologically responsible. Fisherman anchors work well in rocky areas, and CQR and Bruce anchors are a bit less desirable here. Note: Always try to leave the sea bottom the way you found it.

Once the anchor line is cleated, there are a few ways for you to determine how well the anchor is set. First, notice how the vessel is riding to the anchor. If there is some current, and the boat bobs back and forth sharply, like a fish on a hook, there is a good probability that the anchor is holding securely. Second, place your hand on the anchor line, where it leaves the bow. If the anchor is dragging, you will feel a hard shuddering in the line. Water current against the line will make the line vibrate, too. The major difference is that if the anchor is dragging, you will feel the line slacken for a moment and then quickly tighten as the anchor gets a grip. However, if the rode slackens and gently snugs up again, the boat could be just riding forward and back on the rode. Let your hands be your guide.

If the water is warm and clear enough, it is a good idea to send a crew on a snorkel mission to check the set of your anchor.

## Tip 5.10  Allow ample scope

As mentioned earlier, scope is the ratio between the depth of the water in which you are anchoring, and the total length of anchor line and chain (rode) that must be let out. For example, if you are anchored in 10 feet of water, you need 70 feet of rode for a scope of 7 to 1.

The optimum scope is 7 to 1, although 5 to 1 will suffice in places where there are weak currents and the bottom has good holding qualities (mud, for instance). I'll discuss reducing scope in a few more paragraphs.

What is the magic in the 7-to-1 ratio? It provides for a specific angle between the rode (when it is pulled taut) and the seabed. This angle helps drive the anchor downward into the bottom for the best possible bite. Roughly, a scope of 7 to 1 provides a 7-degree angle between the rode and the seabed, a scope of 6 to 1 provides a 9-degree angle, and a scope of 5 to 1 provides an 11-degree angle.

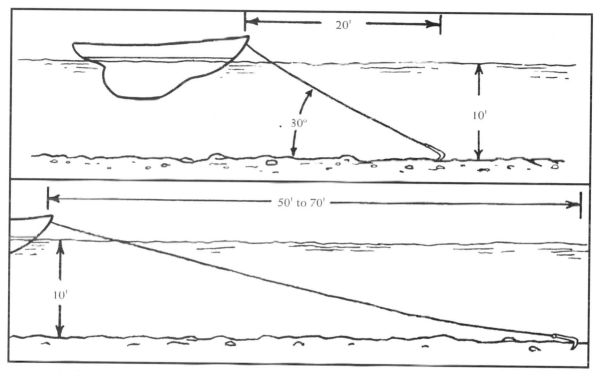

As the scope shortens, there is less opportunity for the anchor to bite into the seabed. A 2-to-1 scope brings the angle between the rode and the seabed to 30 degrees or more and makes it almost impossible for the anchor to dig in.

This corresponds with the angles built into the anchors themselves. CQR anchors are constructed so that the angle between the shank and the plow head is about 30 degrees. Danforth-type anchors have a slightly greater angle, about 32 degrees; while Bruce anchors have a lesser angle of about 15 degrees.

Let's put this in perspective. A scope of 2 to 1 creates a 30-degree angle. If, at that scope, you are trying to set a CQR anchor that itself has a 30-degree head-to-shank angle, then all you are doing is dragging the fluke parallel with the seabed. The anchor's pointed tip isn't going to be in an attitude to bite and hold. You need more scope if the anchor is going to drag nose-down and properly plow into the seabed. (To be fair, CQR anchors offer one benefit in this regard: the crown (head of the anchor) pivots on the shank so it can turn sideways and present a more acute angle to the seabed.)

Here's the how-to of scope in a nutshell. If you are in tight quarters, in an area of minimal currents and wind, and want to restrict your circle of swing (see Tip 5.11) you can use a scope of less than 7 to 1.

But first use a 7-to-1 scope so that your anchor gets a good bite. Then you can shorten the rode. But remember: anything less than 4 to 1 risks the possibility of dragging the anchor.

How do you know how much line you've payed out? There are several ways to mark your chain and rode. These include painting marks at intervals or weaving colored line or vinyl depth markers into the rode. I carry 50 feet of ⅜-inch chain (thus I know the length immediately the chain is payed out) and have colored vinyl strips, marked 75, 100, 125, and so on, threaded through the remaining 150 feet of rode at their respective distances.

## Tip 5.11  Allow for swing

Before you set your anchor, glance around to see whether the approximate amount of anchor line you must let out will leave you with too wide a "swing" (the circle your boat can make around its anchor).

How have the neighboring boats set their anchors? You can judge the amount of scope they have payed out by checking the angle of the anchor line coming from their bows (assuming the line is taut). Choose your position and set your scope so there is no risk of crossing your anchor rode with anyone else's, or of bumping another boat if the vessels were to swing toward one another.

## Tip 5.12  The right way to set an anchor

Anchors usually set themselves, but sometimes they need a little coaxing. The proper procedure calls for the skipper to bring the vessel to a full stop with its bow directly above the point where the anchor is to be set. Then the skipper calls or signals "Ready!" to the crew at the bow, and also calls or signals the water depth so the crew knows how much rode must be payed out for the proper scope (see Tip 5.10).

To make sure another boat will not anchor near, or pass over, this boat's anchor, the skipper has deployed a small buoy to mark the location of the anchor. (Before the anchor is released, one end of a thin line is tied to its crown, the other end to the buoy.)

The crew (wearing gloves, as explained in Tip 5.4) lowers the anchor, and does not throw it. He or she lets the line pay out until the weight of the anchor disappears from the line as it and the chain settle on the bottom. The crew then signals the skipper that the anchor is down, and the skipper begins backing the boat.

As the boat moves astern, the crew puts only one-half turn of line around the bollard or cleat to which the line will be fastened and pays out the line slowly. When almost all the desired scope has been payed out, the crew signals the skipper to stop backing up. As the boat slows, the crew snubs the line by pulling it more firmly against the bollard or cleat. While it is okay at this time to take one whole turn around the bollard or cleat (such that the line can still be slipped free), the line should not be made fast (securely tightened) until the boat has fully stopped its rearward motion. The boat should never be jerked to a halt.

By the way, don't ever try to use your hands and brute force to hold the line. If the boat is larger than a 10-foot dinghy, you can't hold it back. Let the hardware take the load.

To make sure you're paying out the right amount of rode and scope, your anchor line should be marked every 10 feet. Chandlers sell numbered plastic bands that can be woven through the anchor line.

## Tip 5.13  How to handle an anchor by yourself

Anchoring can easily be managed single-handed if you're in calm water, even on a 40-foot or 50-foot boat. Follow these simple steps:

1.  Take your time. There is no need to rush.

2.  If your anchor line will pay out freely from an anchor well or through a chain pipe, or if it was flaked (see Tip 5.3) into a box, you are ready for step 3. However, if the line is stored in a box, and not flaked, now is the time to eliminate all the snags. Remove the line from the box and lay it out on deck so that you can be sure it will pay out without getting snagged. Be sure to tie off the free end of the line to a secure cleat.

3.  Free any lines or devices that secure the anchor.

4.  Bring your boat into position, heading as you wish it to lie when the anchor is set. It will help if you can face the bow into the wind.

5.  Stop the vessel. Go to the bow and drop the anchor until you feel the anchor reach the seabed. Don't cleat the line yet but be sure it's free to pay out.

6.  Return to the helm and put the gear in reverse to begin moving the vessel astern (backward). As soon as it begins to move, put the gear in neutral. Lock the wheel or secure the tiller to its center-mast point.

7.  Return to the bow and let out sufficient rode for the anchor to set, slowing the boat by using the anchor line against the bollard or cleat as described in Tip 5.12. Cleat the line—and watch your fingers. Go back to the helm.

8.  If there was not sufficient propulsion to move the boat far enough to set the anchor, put the gear in reverse again, apply some power until the boat begins to move astern, then move the throttle to idle and shift to neutral. The boat should come to a stop when the anchor sets.

9.  Leave the engine(s) running for a few minutes and allow the boat to come to its natural resting point. This will be determined by wind, currents, and the rode's settling. Turn off the engine(s) only when you are satisfied with your position and you are sure you have ample searoom from the shore, obstructions, and other boats.

Note: Some skippers let out all the necessary anchor rode before going back to the helm to apply reverse thrust to set the anchor. While this can work well, it does present three risks: having line in the water while you are under power; dropping your chain on top of your anchor and possibly snagging it; and jerking the boat to an abrupt halt and possibly breaking the line or cleats.

Weighing an anchor by yourself is just as simple. When leaving a calm-water anchorage, start your engine, then go forward and bring in your anchor line (with the engine in neutral). Whether you weigh the anchor by hand or use a mechanical windlass, take up the line in short hauls. If you are weighing by hand, haul in four or five feet of rode at a time. As you take in line, allow the boat to come forward slowly over the anchor. Trying to hurry just causes a lot of unnecessary work. Once you are over the anchor, you can (1) break it out by hand, (2) hoist it free with the windlass, or (3) cleat the line and then power forward slightly to free the anchor from the seabed.

Once again, take your time. If you are calm you will be able to handle it quite easily. See Tip 5.19 for handling snagged or stubborn anchors.

## Tip 5.14 The right way to set two anchors at the bow

In places where the holding power of the seabed is questionable, or where currents are severe and you need to match the swing of neighboring boats (who also have two anchors set only from their bow), you will need to set two bow anchors. Typically, this means you set your main anchor with normal scope, then set a secondary or backup anchor with almost as much scope as that of the first, using your dinghy.

Begin by setting your first anchor as explained in Tip 5.12. Be sure it is firmly set and not dragging, and that you have sufficient scope. Then get your second anchor ready at the bow, being sure to make fast the bitter end of the line in case it accidentally runs free.

Have a crewmember bring the dinghy forward. Carefully lower the second anchor, its chain, and the line into the dinghy. Take your time. The crewmember in the dinghy must take a moment to flake out the line again, laying out the chain and rode in an orderly fashion, transforming it from the "anchor-first-in" pile that was handed down to a new "anchor-first-out" pile. Remember that line flaked into a pile, bucket, or box will always pay out smoothly without trouble as long as the pile is not disturbed.

Have the crewmember row the dinghy off to port or starboard (rather than directly ahead) as you slowly pay out additional line from the bow going out a distance that is at least five to seven times the water depth, and at an angle of no less than 30 degrees to the right or left of the main anchor. The directions, which can be spotted more easily from the boat, will have to be given (hand signals, again) from the person working at the bow to the crew in the dinghy.

When he or she has gone far enough, signal a halt. (You'll be better positioned to judge if you stay at the bow.) After the crew first makes sure that the line and chain will release freely, the second anchor is lowered overboard.

As it sinks to the bottom and all of the line on the dinghy pays out, you will need to release additional rode from the bow. (Remember your gloves.)

This anchor should be set (dug into the bottom) as well. Cleat off the line to establish a sufficient-scope reference point, then start hauling it in by hand. When the anchor bites home you will feel your boat pulling toward it. But if the anchor continually slips toward you, you will have to send it out again and re-set it. Once the anchor is holding firm, you can let the line out to where you cleated it.

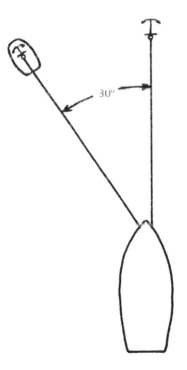

The dinghy heads off 30 degrees to the port or starboard of the main anchor rode, guided by a crewmember on the bow of the anchored boat. Unless a buoy was deployed to mark the location of the original anchor, you need to make a guess as to its distance and location.

You can also set the second anchor from the boat without the help of a dinghy. To do this, you need two crewmembers at the bow and one at the helm. Using hand signals, a crewmember on the bow indicates to the helmsman where to steer. As the boat moves forward, one crew (wearing gloves) takes in any slack in the first anchor's rode to prevent it snagging the propeller. Care must be taken not to disturb the main anchor. Just before the boat arrives over the second anchor's new home, the crewmember at the bow signals the helm to stop so the second anchor can be dropped. Next, signal for the helm to go astern. As the boat backs, the two crew at the bow pay out both rodes. Set the second anchor by hand as described in the previous paragraph.

## Tip 5.15  The right way to set anchors at the bow and stern

There are places where you need your boat to stay in one spot after it's anchored. What sort of places are these? A typical one would be an anchorage along the edge of a river or a slough that's affected by tidal action. Here, the reversals in currents might make a boat that is riding only to a bow anchor swing through 180 degrees, either forcing it against the bank or, at slack water, perhaps leaving it exposed across the channel. Additionally, a 180-degree pull against the anchor would most surely cause it to break out and drag. (In spots where you have a steady river current, though, two bow anchors remain the best configuration.)

Another place, as noted in Tip 5.6, would be wherever you had similarly anchored neighbors. One likely scenario would involve arriving late at an anchorage where everyone else had picked up fore-and-aft moorings, and finding only one mooring ball left. You would need to pick up the remaining ball as your first anchor point, and drop the hook astern for your second.

Let's assume you've either set a bow anchor or tied up (at the bow) to a mooring. Now, how do you secure the stern? If you have enough anchor line and there is a current, the easiest thing is to let out line and drift downstream to the point where you want to set your second anchor, then drop the anchor from the stern. (Power backward if there's no current.)

Once the anchor is down, just power forward but be sure to have a crewmember forward to take in line so it does not float free and get snagged in the prop. Take in the slack in the line until you lie comfortably between both anchors.

If you don't have enough anchor line, or if for some reason you can't work your boat astern, then you can set the stern anchor using your dinghy in virtually the same way as described in Tip 5.14. However, this is a last-resort measure you should reserve for emergencies. Here's why: If your stern anchor is well dug in, the dinghy may not be up to the task of freeing it when you're ready to depart. If you're unable to maneuver your boat back over the anchor, you'll be without a strong enough platform to successfully weigh it. I've seen this situation a dozen times, and it doesn't make for happy skippers.

In a pinch, you could buoy the stern anchor line when you're ready to leave, and cast it off. Then, raise the forward anchor, or slip the mooring, motor up to your buoy, pick up the line, and weigh anchor over the bow roller as usual.

## Tip 5.16 Go slow when you're weighing anchor

Weighing (or raising) an anchor is an exercise in patience. Over the years, I've watched skippers work themselves into frenzies trying to pull up stubborn anchors. But, it doesn't have to be that way. The most successful anchor-weighing technique is always one that looks and feels easy

This crewmember took up slack by hand and waited for the boat to move closer to the anchor. He patiently waited until more slack came into the line and continued the process until he was standing directly over the anchor.

Assuming your anchor line is not snagged under a rock, or hooked around a cable (I've done that myself), you should be able to weigh the anchor with this procedure (see the last section of Tip 5.13 for weighing an anchor while singlehanding):

- Power forward slowly, taking in line and chain as you go, until you are directly above the anchor.

- Once you are over the anchor, cleat the chain or line, leaving little or no slack in it.

- Allow the boat to remain that way for a minute or two. Chances are that the current or the movement of the boat, working against the line or chain at that extreme vertical angle, will break the anchor free. If you're anchored in mud, you'll need special patience, however. Breaking an anchor out of a mud bottom takes extra time.

- Keep a sharp eye on neighboring boats in the anchorage, or other reference points, so you can check your movement. If you begin to drift, you'll know the anchor has come free.

- Once the anchor is free, signal the helmsman to begin moving the boat and getting steerage way. Bring the anchor to the surface, but not yet out of the water. The rush of water against the chain and anchor will wash them clean, so most traces of mud, grass, or sand should be gone before you take the anchor aboard.

- Bring the anchor aboard, secure it, and temporarily stow the chain and line.

- When you get back to the dock, be sure to rinse off the anchor, chain, and line and allow it to dry before stowing it.

## Tip 5.17  Make anchor-handling easy on yourself

Whenever you haul in an anchor line, do so in a sitting position—don't use your back. You'll enjoy the rest of the day a lot more. And when you put away line or chain, always feed it into a contained space or pile that won't be disturbed. If you can keep it isolated like that, then it doesn't matter how spaghetti-like the coils look as the line goes into the container or locker. The line will always pay out just as it went in. But be prepared for trouble if you re-adjust the line in the container, or move the pile; it's certain to snarl or snag when you try to pay it out again.

## Tip 5.18  How to weigh two anchors

The technique of weighing two anchors is virtually the same as that for weighing one anchor. It just requires a little more care.

Begin with your second anchor, hauling in its line and working the boat slowly forward toward the anchor. You should be able to do this by hand; but if you must use the engine, be sure you keep an eye on the main anchor rode: You now have a line in the water that could find its way to the propeller.

Once you're over the second anchor, bring it up as described in Tip 5.16. Then proceed to the main anchor. (As a safety measure, it's a good idea to take in any slack in the main anchor rode to be sure it does not foul the propeller.)

## Tip 5.19  Learn the tricks for freeing a fouled anchor

Fouling an anchor can ruin your day. I know. I once snagged a cable with my anchor in Clipper Cove, at San Francisco Bay's Treasure Island. As I was vainly trying to bring my anchor in, a kindly old salt rowed over my way and said "Hey! You're on the cable."

I yelled back, "I've been coming here for five years, and I don't think there's a cable there."

He retorted, "Well, I've been coming here for 30 years. You're on the cable. Now, when I jump in, slack your chain."

Before I could say, "Are you serious? This is 55-degree water" he was over the side. When he surfaced a moment later, my anchor was free. Now that's what you call sailing camaraderie.

We were in 10 feet of water. If he hadn't come to my rescue, what could I have done? Well, first of all, I could have been better prepared. Today I have a trip line (a second line attached to the crown of my CQR anchor) leading up along with my anchor line. If the anchor gets snagged, I can lower all chain. Then, using the trip line, I have a good chance of being able to pull up the anchor by the crown, with the point and shank facing down.

Second, I now take along a "messenger," a 2-foot length of $\frac{3}{8}$-inch chain carrying a shackle and a 10-pound lead weight.

Here's how to use one:

- Keep tension on the anchor line so that the anchor's shank is pointing upwards.

- Fasten the weighted messenger into a loop around the anchor line. Then attach a separate line to the loop, and lower the loop down the anchor line until it reaches the anchor. The messenger should go down around the anchor's shank, and right up to the crown. Secure the bitter end of the messenger line to a stern or bow cleat (according to how you plan to maneuver).

- Next, drop your anchor line and chain. If you don't have someone in a dinghy to take the free end of the anchor line, coil it (to keep

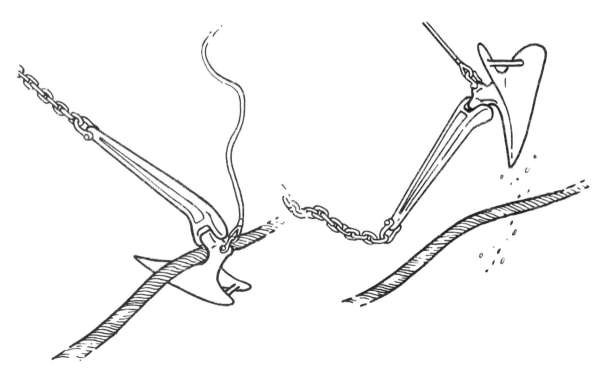

Anchors can find their way to cables, pipes, and other anchor chains. If you keep a trip-line fastened to the crown of your anchor, you can lower your chain and rode and weigh the anchor by its crown.

it in one place) and tie it to a buoy, which can be as simple as a plastic bottle with the lid carefully taped on, or a spare fender.

● Now, free from the anchor, you motor 180 degrees around to the opposite side of the anchor, taking care that you don't get snagged in the free anchor line. Using the messenger's line, and now pulling from the opposite direction you can, with any luck, pull the anchor free by tugging on its crown.

Sometimes an anchor isn't snagged: it's just set very well. In those cases, you may only need an extra measure of power to get it free. Many larger powerboats have motor-driven windlasses that can deliver a good tug on the anchor line. On a sailboat, one trick is to bring the anchor line back from the bow and run it around a winch. In either case, you have to judge carefully how much force you are exerting, and whether the anchor is just dug in well or is actually caught on something.

In most cases, sailboats can sail an anchor out easily enough in a few minutes and a powerboat can do the same, using the boat's mass and momentum to do the work. As an alternative, if you aren't in a hurry and you're anchored in an area that experiences tidal changes of depth, you can have the tides supply your extra lifting power. Secure the anchor line at other than high tide and let nature do the rest. Assuming you're not just entering low tide, be prepared to wait a few hours.

What if the anchor is badly snagged? As a last resort, you may have to dive for it or call a professional diver if the water is too deep or too cold for you. If it comes to the worst, and you have to cut the line and leave the anchor, then you should first make the line as short as possible and tie a plastic bottle or some other kind of buoy to the free end. Don't leave a loose line waving around for some other boat to snag in its propeller. Finally, inform the Coast Guard or local authorities about the location of your abandoned anchor.

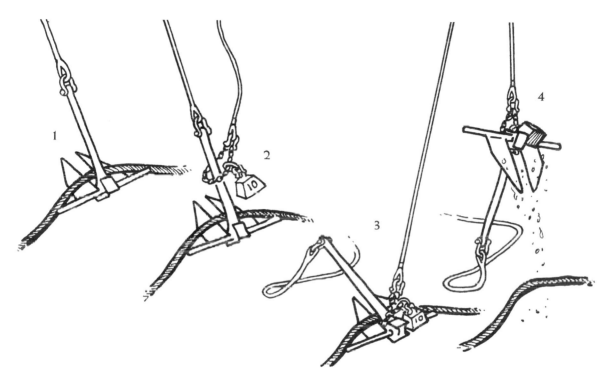

If you don't have a trip-line connected to your anchor, at the very least carry a "messenger," a short length of chain made into a loop with a shackle connector. If you think the anchor is snagged on a cable or pipe then: (1) tighten up on the anchor rode, (2) slide the messenger and its trip-line down the rode until you feel the weight disappear (the messenger slides down the anchor's shank and up to the crown), (3) lower the anchor chain, and (4) pull up on the messenger's trip-line. If the messenger just comes up the anchor rode repeat steps 1 through 3, then hand your trip-line to another boat. Back your boat so that the anchor's shank lies back down at a low angle, then slack the rode, and have the assisting boat pull the anchor free (using the trip-line) from the opposite direction.

## Tip 5.20 How to deal with two fouled anchors

*Two* fouled anchors? Yes, it can and does happen when you set two bow anchors. In fact, it's a very common occurrence and usually the problem is very easy to solve. How do the anchors get fouled? Typically, in one of two ways:

- Your boat swings through 360 degrees during the night, probably more than once.

- The current changes, so that your boat is pulled off at a wide angle, uprooting one of the anchors and dragging it close to the secure anchor.

In either case, you will discover the problem quickly once you begin to raise the anchors. It will be obvious that the lines are tangled. Don't panic. Simply haul in both rodes a little at a time until you are directly over one of the anchors.

Just raise this anchor to the point where you can see it in the water, then cleat the line. If it keeps coming up freely, you should be able to unsnag the crossed line by using a boathook. (You may find that you need to slip one rode over the other to give you working slack.)

If you can't bring up the first anchor because of the way the lines are snagged, then raise the second anchor. If all goes well, they will swing free of each other in the water. At the most, you might have to take the dinghy forward and do some manual untangling at water level. If you don't have a dinghy, you will have to do some creative un-rigging while hanging from your bow. Your boathook may come in handy here.

If you foul your anchor with another boat's anchor line, come alongside, raft up to each other (tie up) and deal with both lines as if you were one boat with two bows. (See Tip 5.22 for some precautions regarding rafting up.)

## Tip 5.21  Picking up a mooring

Often the work of "anchoring" has been done for you, and you need only tie up to a mooring. Moorings are fairly common wherever you may be boating. Most provide a line, already tied to the "ball" or float, that you can snag with a boathook. Others offer a ring to which you can secure your own line.

For picking up moorings, a plastic carry box with the line flaked in (first in, last out) makes all the difference in the world. Note that the "first-in" eye was brought back out of the box and fitted with a carabiner. The carabiner enables a quick attachment back to the main part of the line (forming a loop) in the event the line is not long enough to double up.

Notice those puzzled looks? While trying to set up a quick connection to a mooring, this crew pulled their snagged line from a box and wasted valuable time sorting it out.

Some moorings sport a weighted pole and flag on a "pickup buoy," with a thin "painter" (a short connecting line) going to the mooring line. The flag is high enough for the helmsman to steer to. The pole can be picked up first, and its painter brings in the mooring line.

When you begin your approach to a mooring, your crew should have a boathook ready. Go forward into the wind, with your crew on the bow, using the same hand signals described in Tip 5.7. Having two crew forward is best: one to pick the mooring line straight up in the air, and the other to grab it and quickly make it fast to a cleat. With a little practice, you can easily pick up moorings if you are singlehanding. The key is to take your time and prepare all pickup lines and tools ahead of time.

You may need to remind your crew that boathooks are meant only for picking up lines and are not strong enough to be used as pry bars to muscle lines around a stanchion or over the rail.

If you are tying to the ring of a mooring ball, you can find several devices on the market that attach to the end of a pole, and will allow you to clamp the line automatically to and through the ring. Of course, you can use a boathook to grab the ring and hold the ball, but then you still have the problem of getting your line through the ring.

My advice, especially if you're singlehanding, is to approach the mooring ball so it comes along the hull and back toward the stern. That's where your freeboard (the distance between the boat's deck and the water) is lowest. You merely reach over, slip the line through the ring and walk the line forward to the bow cleat, pulling the bow and ball toward each other as you go. Either of these steps is safe, easy, and has the extra advantage of making you look like an old salt. You can also have a line already made up from the bow cleat, through the roller, outside the lifelines, and back to the cockpit. Then you simply bring the buoy alongside at cockpit level, slip the line through the ring, and you're moored.

## Tip 5.22  Know the etiquette of rafting up

Rafting, the practice of tying up side-by-side with another vessel, is common in many anchorages, especially when vessels are there for short stays. Pulling up to a vessel when rafting is much like pulling up to a dock. The chief differences are that (usually) someone is aboard the waiting vessel, able to receive dock lines; and you need to exercise special care so you don't bang into the boat on your approach.

When rafting up to another boat, have your fenders ready. Secure fenders high and at the point of widest beam to keep boats and their caprails far apart.

Three or four boats can make fast to commercial moorings. If there is not a commercial mooring available, at least two bow anchors should be set for a raft-up like this and, if there is no current, a stern anchor will keep the entire raft from turning.

Here are some rafting pointers:

- Vessels should be well protected by fenders. Use large fenders, big enough to keep the caprails (wooden edgings at the intersection of the hull and deck) from striking each other in a surge. (See Tip 1.6.)

- It's a good idea to use as many shock-absorbing devices in the lines as possible. Most marine stores carry line "snubbers" that minimize shock as the vessels are jostled against one other by the current and wave surge. It is generally better to keep the springlines (lines that go diagonally from the bow of one boat to the stern of the other) tight so that the boats are held together (with fenders between) rather than leaving the lines loose and allowing the boats to bang into one another.

- Never tie fenders to the lifelines: If one fender gets caught between the boats in a heavy swell, the downward load could break the lifelines or bend stanchions.

- If you must tie a line to a stanchion (which you should try to avoid doing), be sure to tie it to the base of the stanchion, not to the top, or head.

- With rafted sailboats, be sure that springlines, which prevent forward and backward movement, are used in aligning the boats so that the spreaders won't bang into each other when the vessels rock.

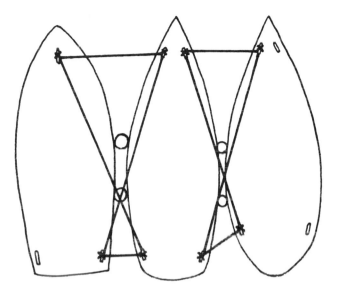

Springlines are a must when rafting up. As in docking (Tip 3.12), springlines keep boats in their proper positions. This is especially important for sailboats, so that their spreaders do not collide when the boats roll in opposite directions.

In areas of little or no current, springlines can be loosely fitted. If there is substantial current or constant wakes from nearby traffic, tie rafted boats snugly to keep them from banging into each other.

## Chapter 6

# DINGHIES

One would think that the most likely time to lose a dinghy is when one is as relaxed as a hound dog, cruising idly under a warm sun in the crystal-blue water of the magnificent British Virgin Islands, never looking astern to see if one's dinghy is still there. Maybe. But that's not when we lost ours.

In this book's preface, I spoke of my reunion with an old sailing pal, Captain Stu. Well, we temporarily lost our dinghy that night. It had been tied to his boat as we sat at anchor, reminiscing and carefully evaluating some of the local rum. The wind was howling, causing the dinghy to tug relentlessly at the painter. Eventually, the knot slipped loose and so did the dinghy. It can get amazingly dark in Marina Cay, where there are no lights to mark the shoreline, especially during a new moon and with heavy overcast. Pitch blackness doesn't adequately describe the visibility, or lack thereof, that night.

How we found the dinghy is a great story. A 15-minute search mission with two flashlights and Stuart's dinghy turned up nothing. As we followed the channel out to the open sea, all we found was a lot of wind, water, and darkness. Captain Stuart had the solution: we went back to his boat, shut off his outboard, and allowed his dinghy to drift in the current and wind, attempting to recreate the path of my dinghy. There, 15 minutes later as we drifted towards the shore, sitting on a quiet bank more than a mile away, just waiting to be found, was our dinghy. Voilà!

Dinghies are just little utility boats, it's true. But they represent money out of your pocket, and they carry cargo and people that are important to you. So be good to them and protect your investment.

## Tip 6.1 Extend your dinghy's life with proper storage

If you have an inflatable dinghy, keep it airtight and dependable by giving it proper care. Hose it off with fresh water after you use it, then let it dry, deflate it, fold it carefully, and stow it out of the sun.

Spend a few moments cleaning the threads of all air-valve fittings, and lubricate them occasionally with petroleum jelly. These steps may sound obvious, but it's amazing how many boat owners neglect them, and so take months or years off a dinghy's life.

## Tip 6.2 Treat your dinghy's skin as you would your own

I once saw a diver surface after a spearfishing expedition and literally *throw* his speargun into his inflatable dinghy before climbing in after it. People who do that must either have lots of money to spend on new inflatables, or like to swim. If you use tools, fishing gear, or anything sharp, pointed, or angular anywhere near an inflatable dinghy, be careful. The skin you puncture may be your dinghy's, but the cost of fixing or replacing it comes out of your hide.

## Tip 6.3 Double-tie your dinghy

Always double-tie your painter (the line you use to secure the dinghy to your boat or dock). That means when you make your first knot, leave yourself enough extra line to tie another knot at a second point. A lone knot can come loose even in the best of conditions.

Another solution is to attach a stainless-steel snap shackle to the painter so that you can secure the painter around a cleat or stanchion and then snap the line back onto itself.

Finally, don't forget that your painter has two ends. Check the attachments on the dinghy as well. Are the knots secure? Are the D-rings or attachments on the dinghy securely fastened? Is the painter rubbing on something that might fray or cut it?

## Tip 6.4 Distribute the payload

No matter what kind of dinghy you use, you should always try to keep the weight of any passengers and gear distributed evenly in it. Seat a passenger forward whenever possible, because your best speed, stability, and steering control come when the dinghy is riding flat, whether you have a hard dinghy or an inflatable one. This adjustment may be tricky when you are the sole passenger, but make a point of putting fuel tanks or any extra payload well forward. While it may seem racy to have your dinghy planing like a speedboat, it will handle better and more safely if you keep its nose to the water.

Don't overload your dinghy and be sure that the payload is well distributed. Be sure there are floatable cushions or life preservers in the dinghy before you depart.

### Tip 6.5  Carry the right gear

Whenever you're on the water, be sure your dinghy carries a complement of basic gear. This should include tools you need to repair the outboard (including extra spark plugs), sufficient spare fuel, life preservers (one per person), a handheld VHF radio in a waterproof pouch, and a flashlight. The purposes are self-evident. Your dinghy is a utility craft, true enough; but the most useful thing it may ever do is save your life in an emergency.

This young boater is getting a good workout at the oars. More importantly, she's well prepared with a life vest.

## Tip 6.6 Entering and leaving the dinghy

When you're entering the dinghy, gently place your weight in the middle. Do not jump, leap, swing, or flop. Never transfer your weight into it suddenly. The smoother the transition you make from vessel to dinghy, or from dock to dinghy, the less chance there will be for tipping the craft, losing your own balance, or endangering other passengers.

Leave the dinghy just as smartly. Step from the dinghy to your boat or to the dock with a smooth motion, shifting your weight forward and up. Rise on the exiting foot; don't push off from the foot that is still in the dinghy. The dinghy isn't on pavement, it's on water, and it will obligingly go where it's pushed, giving you an opportunity to swim when you may have had something quite different in mind.

(1) Step into the dinghy while holding on to the boat, and then immediately transfer your grip to the dinghy. Standing up without holding on is the first step toward swimming. (2) Stay low and centered, and immediately sit down. (3) When leaving, step up and pull your weight out of the dinghy. Don't push off—the force will push the dinghy away from the boat, making it harder to disembark.

### Tip 6.7 Ease the strain on a dinghy under tow

Towing puts a considerable strain on a dinghy's painter as well as on its pad-eyes or D-rings. Take care with these attachments, no matter whether your dinghy is an inflatable or a small skiff.

Spread the strain around. The more places you can attach the painter to, the better. It also is good practice to have extra line attached to a secondary ring, just in case the first connection parts.

Regardless of the kind of dinghy you are towing, try to have it ride just in front of the crest of your yacht's stern wave. That is, pay out enough line so the dinghy rides on your side of the wave behind your vessel's stern. This way, the dinghy will follow with the lightest load on its line and connection points.

### Tip 6.8 Towing a payload doesn't pay

Even though storage space usually is at a premium on a boat, especially during long cruises, resist the temptation to carry an extra payload in your dinghy. The dinghy has a hard enough time being tugged by a painter. Don't give it an additional burden. You run a risk of flipping the dinghy and losing your cargo. For that matter, the extra weight increases your chances of having the painter break, costing you both payload and dinghy.

### Tip 6.9 Mind the capacity

All vessels are designed for a maximum payload and in the case of commercially made dinghies or skiffs, the number of maximum passengers is usually stamped or labeled somewhere on the boat. It is not a question of available seats, but of buoyancy—the ability of the vessel to support its payload. To exceed this limit is to invite trouble or disaster.

## Tip 6.10  Will your dinghy stop when you do?

As you slow your boat for docking and close maneuvering, the dinghy will have a mind of its own unless you take steps to control it first. A free-floating hard dinghy can do damage if it slams into the stern of your boat. And the dinghy's painter will undoubtedly find its way to your propeller, especially if you are in reverse.

Before reducing speed or stopping, have a crew member pull the dinghy up to your vessel so that the two are in contact before you reduce speed. This also gets extra painter out of the water, safe from getting fouled. If the dinghy is wood or aluminum, place a fender between it and your boat.

For mooring or rafting up, bring the dinghy close alongside the side away from the other vessel, and tie it to a cleat or stanchion

## Chapter 7

# BOATKEEPING

I have been fortunate to find all major problems before they found me. But I didn't find them by accident. I keep a maintenance log and routinely perform inspections to ensure that all mechanical and electrical devices are in good working order.

I changed the shrouds (the sailboat's mast cables) when they reached the suggested 10 years of maturity; ground the valves and replaced head gaskets on my Volvo diesel because I thought it was time. I remove and inspect the exhaust header every five years. And, when not working from my log, I look for loose bolts, rusted parts, frayed wires, bad connections, hardened hoses, and more. Sometimes, I'll just crawl into a spot and lie there looking for trouble.

Most importantly, I know my boat like the back of my hand and I think she likes the attention.

Technology has yet to bring us to the age of the self-maintaining boat. In the meantime, it is up to you to make sure your boat stays safe, comfortable, and seaworthy. Spending some time with a wrench in your hand will mean more worry-free hours spent with the tiller or the wheel in your hand. As investments go, that's a very good deal.

## Tip 7.1 Inspect everything

Although there are more moving parts in a car, a boat can be stopped just as dead in its tracks because of something that loosens. And what passes for "normal wear and tear" outside the marine environment is greatly accelerated by water, salt, and sun. The best advice: regularly check everything.

Common trouble spots in the engine compartment are the propeller shaft's mating flange bolts and set-screws; gearshift and throttle linkages; fuel connections; oil and fuel filters; engine mounts; and propeller nuts. Steering linkages and cables also loosen, as do electrical connectors attached to the various instruments and controls. Winches wear, as do steering gears and sheaves (pulleys). The pins on snap shackles can wear. Lines (ropes) wear. Check everything.

Things that loosen will break. Things that wear will break. Things that are poorly made or poorly designed will break. Often, things that are poorly used will break. While most marine parts are well made, if they are sized improperly, applied to the wrong purpose, or stressed at the wrong angle, they can be damaged. Some failures are preventable if you're early enough in discovering stressed parts, corrosion, worn materials, or thin hairline cracks. Corrosion around welds often is a sign of impending failure. Among all the things that loosen, wear, or break, things that break due to structural failure can be the most difficult to discover during routine maintenance. So check everything.

Keep an assortment of nonrusting tools aboard, as well as extra bulbs, bolts, fasteners, cotter pins, cotter rings, a spool of whipping line, and some stainless-steel safety wire. If you are a neophyte mechanic, check the bookshelf in your local marine store and purchase a few good books on marine maintenance, familiarize yourself with their contents, and keep them on your boat.

Outboard engines provide the great advantage of being portable and allowing you to take them home for flushing with fresh water, storage away from salt water, routine maintenance, and closer inspection.

Keep an extra fuel filter, oil filter, and extra oil on board. Of course, the necessary seals and O-rings should accompany the filters.

Prepare a checklist of serviceable items (see Tip 7.20) and establish some dates for routine inspection. Make several copies of the checklist and keep track of the dates and services performed in your new "log."

## Tip 7.2  Care for your lifelines, shrouds, and halyards

Don't take lines for granted. As part of your regular preventive maintenance, be sure that your lifelines and related fittings are in good working order, and that all cotter pins and cotter rings are securely fitted. Sharp-ended cotter pins should be taped over to keep them from catching clothes, skin and sails.

You can find barbs in stainless-wire rope by rubbing tissue paper along the wire. The barbs will catch the tissue, thus flagging broken strands. Broken strands are a sign of stressed and deteriorating wire. Change it. Check rope-to-wire connections for signs of rope wear and loose rope strands. If you have any doubts, change the lines. And, by all means, if you have any doubts about your rope-to-wire splices on halyards, don't use the halyards to haul a crewmember aloft in a bosun's chair.

Inspect rigging fittings and shackles for signs of hairline cracks, which are common to swaged fittings—those where a stainless steel fitting is pressed around stainless-steel wire. For safety, a sailboat's standing rigging should be changed at least once every 10 years.

## Tip 7.3  Dry lines properly, store them out of the sun

Dock lines, anchor lines, and halyards deteriorate and cause odors if you put them away wet. And, if they have been waterlogged with salt water, when they dry they become crusted with salt, are more difficult to handle, and begin to smell.

Hose them off with fresh water on your return to harbor. Allow them to dry before you stow them. If they must go into a locker while wet, be sure the locker is well ventilated.

If the lines are small enough, consider taking them home occasionally and running them through your washing machine with a mild detergent (think of an excuse in case your mate asks you why the kids' clothes smell like dead fish). Then let them air dry. It will leave them clean, pliable, and easy to work.

Regardless of the composition of the lines you are using, exposure to sunlight will shorten their working life. As much as possible, store lines out of the sun when they aren't in use. It's best to hang them in a locker or open space, rather than piling them where they cannot get air to dry.

## Tip 7.4  Don't let your lines pick up splinters

When you're drying lines at the marina, always try to lay them out on your deck or on a concrete dock or walkway. If you dry lines on a wooden dock, they often pick up little slivers of wood when you haul them in—eager to become splinters in your hands, or the hands of your crew.

## Tip 7.5  Check your boat's steering linkage often

There are basically three kinds of steering systems:

1. Direct mechanical connections, such as tillers and rack-and-pinion wheel systems.

2. Transferred mechanical systems, such as chain-, cable-, and push/pull wire-driven systems.

3. Hydraulic systems.

   While the most mechanically secure types are the direct mechanical systems, all are prone to fail when fittings (mechanical or hydraulic) work loose, or when chains and cables wear. Mechanical steering systems need to be lubricated on a regular basis. Turning sheaves—pulleys where cables change direction—should be greased, and the pins and bushings inspected annually. Also be sure to check the tightness of all supports and brackets that hold your steering gear in place.

## Tip 7.6  Defend your boat against oxidation

Salt and sun make a difficult environment for even the toughest metals. Not all grades of stainless steel are corrosion-proof. Some of the most commonly used grades still oxidize. Bronze is widely used as marine metal because it resists corrosion. Aluminum sees a lot of marine service because it is less expensive to cast and polish than other metals, but it oxidizes badly and is prone to galvanic corrosion, especially when in contact with another metal, such as stainless steel.

Beyond simple oxidation or rust, when certain metals are exposed to each other in a salt-water environment they become victims of galvanic corrosion (electrolysis).

Anti-corrosion, di-electric compound should be used on steel screws that secure aluminum fittings. Heat-shrink tubing was used around the shafts and heads of these stainless-steel screws to prevent corrosion in this aluminum steering-wheel pedestal.

Metals that are lower on the galvanic scale corrode more readily than do those further up the scale. An aluminum cleat, for example, corrodes faster when secured with stainless screws (the damage is most pronounced around the screw holes). To inhibit this process, it's a good idea to coat fasteners with a di-electric (anti-seizing) compound and, if possible, keep the parts dry (a difficult thing to do in the marine environment). The di-electric compound slows down corrosion and makes it easier to loosen screws later, if you need to remove them. Unfortunately, the compound cannot completely stop or prevent electrolysis.

Incidentally, heat-shrink tubing placed around machine screws and around part of the head on oval-head or flathead machine screws will work wonders to resist corrosion as long as the screw will still fit through the hole. (But, you'll have to tighten the nut rather than the screw so you don't tear the tubing.)

Bronze propellers, bronze through-hull fittings and aluminum engine parts will corrode quickly in salt water if there is an electrical reaction between the metal parts and the surrounding water. However, you can slow down this process, too. Most important is bonding all fittings by wiring them together, and using zinc fittings on propeller shafts and inside the engine's cooling chambers. Zinc becomes a sacrificial metal in the process. Lower in the pecking order of metals, it gives itself up to the more noble metals, thereby sparing from corrosion the shaft and propeller to which it is attached.

General rules to follow are:

- Always use anti-seizing (di-electric) compounds on threads, especially where stainless-steel screws are threaded into aluminum (see Tip 7.9). Consider the heat-shrink tubing idea where applicable.

- Check zincs and replace corroded ones frequently (see Tip 7.10).

- Never use ordinary hardware-store steel screws, nuts, washers or bolts anywhere on your vessel. Parts should only be held together with corrosion-proof fasteners.

- Electrical wire-ends often corrode to the point where the resistance in the connection causes devices to stop working, so put rubber silicone sealer around crimp fittings after you attach them to the wire.

- If you are connecting to existing wires and they appear black when you strip the covering away, clean or scrape away the black oxidized surface before making the new connection.

- Check all of your electrical connections from time to time to see that corrosion has not grown between the contact points of the connection. Scrape away any corrosion, reconnect and cover the connection with a protective coating (di-electric grease over a screw-on attachment, and silicone sealant over a crimped one).

## Tip 7.7  Keep an eye on stainless-steel bolts in wet conditions

There are several types of stainless steel, and some actually stain more than others. Most marine-grade stainless steel is the type that resists corrosion, but it is still a good idea to check stainless-steel hose clamps and fasteners that are constantly submerged in sea water. They're corrosion-resistant, not corrosion-proof. Some cheap stainless-steel hose clamps have regular-steel screws; don't use them. If you're the least suspicious about their structural integrity, replace them with new marine-grade stainless-steel equivalents.

### Tip 7.8  Let stainless steel breathe

Stainless steel needs air. Moisture trapped between stainless steel and any rubber or tape that covers it can lead to severe corrosion. Remove tape often to check shrouds and fittings that have these kinds of coverings. And don't cover stainless steel at all if you don't have to. A piece of tape around a stainless-steel stanchion or post can cause more corrosion than you can imagine.

### Tip 7.9  Use anti-seizing (di-electric) compounds with stainless steel and aluminum

The electrolysis problem described in Tip 7.6 comes into sharp focus the minute you try to remove a stainless-steel screw that has spent several months holding an aluminum part in place. Unless the parts were originally coated with a di-electric or anti-seizing compound, removal of the screw can be next to impossible, and more often, completely impossible.

Always use an anti-seizing compound when threading stainless screws into other stainless parts; and use it around the heads of stainless screws that go through aluminum fittings. In fact, apply it wherever stainless and aluminum fasteners touch.

There is one exception to this rule: Do not use an anti-seizing compound on electrical connections, because it inhibits electrical conductivity. Use silicone rubber sealant *over* the completed connection, instead.

## Tip 7.10 Change your sacrificial zincs regularly

We talked about electrolysis in Tip 7.6. Electrolysis is accelerated by dis-similarities between various metals on the boat, and by the presence of stray electrical energy found in most saltwater marinas. What this usually leads to is corroded propellers, propeller shafts, struts, through-hull fittings, engines, and so on.

As I mentioned earlier, pieces of zinc are used in these places to slow down the corrosion process. The zinc gets eaten away (we say it is sacrificed) instead of neighboring metals because it is lower on the galvanic scale.

Divers can be hired to clean boat bottoms and change zincs on outdrives and propeller shafts. Engine zincs can be changed easily from inside the boat. Keep a meticulous schedule for changing zincs, and do so faithfully. It's much cheaper than changing props.

As far as boats that stay in the water are concerned, when you haul your boat to renew the bottom paint, which you should do at least once every 18 months, have the yard check your through-hull fittings for corrosion. If there's any doubt about their integrity, change them. All through-hull fittings should be bonded by connecting them directly to the electrical system's ground. Further, it is preferable that each through-hull fitting should be connected separately to the ground block rather than one fitting being connected to the next, and then to the ground. And, check the accumulation of old paint and corrosion around engine-water-intake strainers that might be causing a restriction. Scrape away any residue before the next coat of bottom paint is applied.

## Tip 7.11  Always use top-quality fuel filters

Diesel fuel and gasoline used in marine environments often contain debris that can stall an engine. Besides the algae that commonly grow in diesel fuel, both gasoline and diesel usually are kept in tanks that are subject to corrosion and are prone to collecting moisture.

Early strainer-type fuel filters used to do a poor job of filtering out minute particles or debris, and an even poorer job of separating out large particles of rust and algae from the fuel. Fortunately, modern filter systems with removable filter cartridges can remove particles as small as 2 microns, and they usually have containment bowls to collect larger particles and separate any residual water.

Have the best fuel filter systems installed on your boat. It's a small price to pay to keep your engine in good health and insure that you, your family and your crew will get home on time from every trip.

Fuel filters should be changed every 200 hours.

If you have diesel power, be sure to use a chemical additive each time you add new fuel. These biocide treatments are designed to reduce fungi in the fuel and keep injectors from clogging.

## Tip 7.12  Change the plugs

If your boat has a gasoline engine with standard ignition, make it a habit to regularly change, not just gap, the points and plugs. Ignition systems on gasoline engines should be changed every season or 300 hours, whichever comes first (change ignition wires every three years). Do this on schedule to prevent fouling and to keep the plugs' threads free from rust. Note the dates and/or engine hours in your log. (Note: Many newer gasoline engines feature electronic ignition, which does not have points.)

## Tip 7.13  Change the oil

Engines last longer when their oil is fresh and clean. It's most important that fresh, clean lubricant gets to all bearing surfaces, and that sludge doesn't build up in oil passages. The lubricating oil in gasoline engines has a limited lifespan. The acidic by-products of combustion in diesel engines render oil ineffective after about 50 hours of operation. (Install an hour-meter if you don't already have one.) As with using good fuel filters (Tip 7.11), regularly changing oil and oil filters—at least every 50 hours of operation for diesel and 100 hours for gasoline engines—is cheap insurance.

Consider the alternative. Removing an engine from a boat to perform a major overhaul often requires elaborate surgery on the boat's woodwork and/or cockpit floor. This process is expensive and disruptive. You can avoid it if you're conscientious about routinely scheduled oil changes and note the dates and engine hours in your log. Be sure to dispose of used oil properly.

## Tip 7.14  Protect all electrical connections

Keep all wires in your vessel's bilge area as high and as dry as possible. Even though marine wire has a durable, seemingly waterproof covering, don't push your luck. Keep it out of the water. Water that gets into wire, especially at the connections, will soak up a long way under the insulation. It won't be long before the wire is rendered useless or incapable of carrying its intended load.

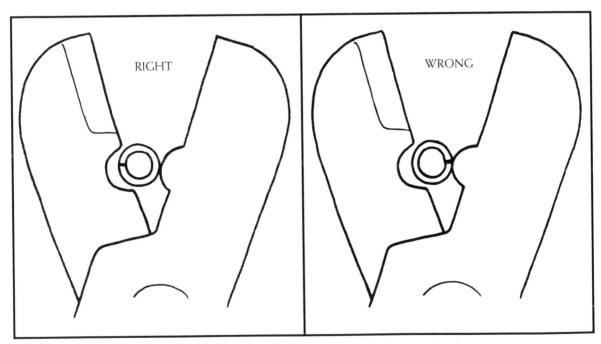

There is a right way and wrong way to crimp wire connectors. The tunnel in the connector is bent metal and has a split where the two ends come together. Put the split into the cradle side of the crimping tool, or else the seam may open and the wire will not be securely held.

When making wire connections anywhere on the boat, especially in the bilge area, use crimp-connectors. Do not twist the wires together and do not use household-type wire nuts. Whenever possible, use soldered connections. Afterward, cover the connections with silicone sealer to keep water out.

## Tip 7.15  Use care when you hose off varnish remover

Maintaining brightwork (finished woodwork) is one of those chores that comes with owning a boat. That means you occasionally need to use varnish remover on your teak. No matter what kind of remover and neutralizer you use, you will undoubtedly do the final wash-off with water. Do that carefully. You want to avoid splattering other boats in the yard, or other parts of your boat.

You should be aware that in most U.S. marinas it's against environmental regulations to hose off varnish remover and similar chemicals into the water. You must first use a neutralizer, then dry off with cloth or paper that you deposit in the trash. Even if you do this ashore in a boatyard, the debris must be contained and properly disposed of. It's the law.

## Tip 7.16  Mask off painted areas when doing brightwork

Many common varnish removers will stain or cause streaking on the gelcoat (the outer coating on your fiberglass) or on a painted surface, especially if it's a dark color. Unless you like the mottled look, before you start on your brightwork, mask off all the adjacent areas that you want to protect. Use regular masking tape and lightweight plastic dropcloths. To protect your topsides (the upper portion of the hull) let the dropcloths extend right down to the boot stripe.

## Tip 7.17  Fire extinguishers are a must

The Coast Guard requires that boats up to 26 feet in length, with enclosed spaces, must have at least one B-1 extinguisher. Boats from 26 to 40 feet must carry two B-1 or one B-2 extinguisher, and boats from 40 to 65 feet must carry three B-1 or one B-1 and one B-2. Be sure to check with your local marine dealer for brands and models that satisfy these ratings.

You should have an automatic extinguisher in the engine compartment (or a regular extinguisher near your engine if it's an outboard), an extinguisher near the stove, another in the forward cabin, and one near the cockpit.

Halon used to be recommended for engine-compartment fire extinguishers. Halon and carbon dioxide are dust-free, heavier than air and can smother a fire quickly. Like carbon dioxide, halon leaves no residue and therefore does little or no damage to electrical or engine components.

Both gases are perfect for stopping a fire and leaving neighboring equipment in working order. Unfortunately, it is believed that halon destroys the ozone layer, so it is now only available for filling extinguishers as a recycled gas, making halon extinguishers very expensive—but well worth the investment. All extinguishers should be fully charged, with up-to-date inspection tags.

While carbon dioxide and halon are clean, they are not recommended for all classes of fires. Dry chemical extinguishers are the runners-up, but they leave a mess. Regardless of the clean-up issue, though, the most important point is to get the fire out fast.

There are four classes of fires, and each responds best to particular extinguishers:

*Class A.* Ordinary combustible materials; wood, paper, cloth, plastics, and so on. Use water or dry chemicals (carbon dioxide might blow light-burning materials around).

*Class B.* Burning liquids such as gasoline, oil, kerosene, alcohol, diesel fuel, paint, lacquer, and so on. Use dry chemicals, halon or carbon dioxide (water might spread the burning liquid).

*Class C.* Electrical fires, where the source of the heat is an electrical connection. The fire can be either the electric equipment itself or surrounding Class-A material that has also caught on fire. Disconnect the circuit. Use dry chemicals, halon or carbon dioxide. Do not use water—it presents the hazard of electrocution.

*Class D.* Metal fires such as aluminum parts, or chemical fires such as the phosphorous used in flares. Get the burning material overboard.

## Tip 7.18 Flashlights are a must, too

As mentioned in Tip 1.1, flashlights (in working order, of course) are essential boating tools. Aside from assisting you at night, a good flashlight will help you find an item dropped into a dark bilge. Like extinguishers, you should have a few that are strategically placed about your boat.

A headband-type flashlight is a great help when you're working on an engine or in restricted spaces. And, to be sure that light is always at your fingertips, a fresh supply of batteries, in sealed bags, should be close at hand.

## Tip 7.19 Life-preserver requirements

You are required to carry the right number of life preservers of the right types. If you operate a vessel between 16 and 65 feet in length, you must have an approved Type I, II, III, or V life preserver on board for each passenger, as well as one Type IV throwable device.

A "life preserver" as defined by Coast Guard regulations is a device that can be worn (as opposed to being held). In 1997, the Coast Guard and the Underwriters Laboratory (UL) approved manually activated models of inflatable vests (which are generally more comfortable to wear).

Here are the five categories of life preservers:

*Type I. Offshore Life Jacket.* Has a minimum of 22 pounds of buoyancy, will turn the wearer face-up and is worn like a vest, with flotation on the back and over the chest area.

*Type II. Near-Shore Life Vest.* Typically the least expensive type of PFDs (personal flotation devices), it provides 15.5 pounds of buoyancy and is worn like collar, with flotation behind the head and over the chest area.

*Type III. Water-Ski Vests.* Designed with specific belts and straps, two of which must encircle the chest.

*Type III. Float Coats.* A subset of the Type III Water-Ski Vests, but with a flotation device sewn into a jacket or coat-like apparel.

*Type III. Inflatable Vests.* Inflatables outperform the foam-filled vests, but the Coast Guard has classified them as Type III because they do not provide flotation unless they are inflated. Inflatables are more comfortable to wear because there is little bulk until they are inflated.

*Type IV. Throwable device.* Intended to be tossed to a victim in the water, the cushion-type of flotation aid provides 18 pounds of buoyancy, the horse-collar-type provides 20 pounds.

*Type V. Special-Use Device.* Typically made of soft foam flotation material, and designed for specific marine work activities.

The regulations specify that Type I, II, and III PFDs must be readily accessible. The Type IV throwable device also must be immediately available.

## Tip 7.20 The checklist

Just to prime your pump, here is a beginning checklist that you may wish to copy and add to:

- **Batteries**: every 6 months, check electrolyte level and top off with distilled water. Also every 6 months, remove terminal fittings, scrape away corrosion on the terminals, and replace the fittings. Replace batteries every 5 years.
- **Bolts, screws**: every 6 months, check tightness of engine mounts, steering components, rudder supports, throttle and shift linkage, check for rust, and discard and replace rusted hardware.
- **Deck fittings**: every 6 months, check screws, tighten, replace screws and nuts, check backing plates, remove rust from stainless stanchions.
- **Electrical connectors**: once a year, inspect wires and replace if loose or corroded. Scrape wires clean and seal the open ends of connectors.
- **Engine(s)**: every 2 months, check hose clamps, look for corroded or rusted bolts, replace engine zincs, and check engine mounts.
- **Fuel filter**: every 50 hours, replace filter and drain residue from bowl.
- **Hose clamps**: once a year, replace if rusted and don't re-use. Fit two clamps on every hose end below the waterline.
- **Lines**: as often as needed, whip loose or frayed ends, check eyes, replace all damaged or heavily chafed lines, and install protective covers where lines can be chafed.

- **Oil and filter:** replace both every 50 hours (for diesel engine) or 100 hours (for gasoline engine).

- **Plugs and plug wires:** every 6 months, inspect plug gaps, adjust if necessary.

- **Radio wiring:** every 6 months, check for frayed or rusted VHF connectors, check wire-to-antenna connection, clean.

- **Rope-to-wire splices:** every 6 months, check for fraying and replace if frayed. (Do not haul crew up mast with badly frayed rope-to-wire connections.)

- **Running lights:** check every time they're used, change if out; carry spare lamps.

- **Spark plugs:** every 12 months, replace; replace corroded wires.

- **Stuffing box:** as often as needed, check the drip rate. There should be virtually no drip when the shaft is still, and a slow steady drip when it is turning. Snug up the packing gland (with engine off) as required and tighten the lock nut.

- **Through-hull fittings:** once a year, check condition out of water. Replace if pitted or corroded. Bronze fittings should not flake when scraped with knife.

- **Trailer fittings:** every 2 months, check tightness of brackets, and repack wheel bearings.

- **Wire halyards:** every year, rub with tissue paper and watch for tissue sticking to wire barbs. Replace wire if it's barbed. Change shrouds every 10 years, barbed or not.

- **Zincs:** every 2 months, change if corroded away.

## Chapter 8

# BOATING AT NIGHT

I was in a deep sleep in my bunk, resting easily in smooth rolling seas on a clear but moonless night. We were about halfway into a 75-mile passage, motoring a sailboat from Santa Cruz to San Francisco for the popular Windjammer race. Our crew of four included a young man who had his sea legs, but needed some fine-tuning. It was his watch, and his partner was below preparing hot chocolate and a snack.

Somewhere beyond the cadence of the diesel engine, I dreamed I heard several snorts of a sea horn. When I dreamed them again, I counted five short blasts.

It was no dream. As my senses and experiences said "Wake up," the blasts were repeated, but this time they vibrated the hull of our Santa Cruz 40. Half-awake, I darted through the companionway and turned to see a stack of three white lights above a blur of cabin lights, and a red bow light 100 yards dead ahead. I literally dove on the tiller, unclipping the pilot and pushing the stick hard to port in one motion. We veered violently to starboard and were quickly moving clear of the crossing tug's path. I heard things crash in the cabin (it turned out later to be the hot chocolate) followed by a stream of foul language.

Our young crew at the helm was startled. "I was passing well behind him," he said angrily, "and he had right of way." But "well behind that tug," I explained, was a barge which, while I didn't see it when I first came on deck, did barely show its running lights.

"I saw the other boat," he said, "but I didn't know it was a barge." In his judgment, he felt we had plenty of room to pass between the two vessels. And, considering only the distance, he might have made it. What he missed was what the three vertical lights should have told him: This was a tug whose overall length, including its tow, was in excess of 200 meters. Had he known that, he would also have realized that the submerged cable between the tug and tow on that dark night could have inflicted severe damage on our boat, or even sunk us.

Should you shy away from boating at night? Absolutely not. Frankly, I think it is exhilarating. Making a passage at night can be just as safe as, if not safer than, making it in broad daylight. Once you're familiar with the system of navigation lights used at night, I think you'll agree.

## Tip 8.1  Learn the night recognition lighting system

Lights are required for boating between sunset and sunrise, or whenever visibility is reduced for any reason. The basic lights you need to recognize are sidelights, sternlights, anchor lights, and masthead or "steaming" lights.

These lights identify the type of vessel carrying them, which way it is heading, whether it is under power or sail, and who has the right of way. Then there are various combinations of additional lights that help to identify the size of a vessel, and what it is doing on the water. (See some basic terms, beginning on page 183.)

Here is an overview of the basic lighting configurations:

A red light is attached to the port bow, a green light is attached to the starboard bow, and a white light is attached to the stern.

Your red port light tells oncomers on your port side to stop or pass behind you—you are the "stand-on" (hold your position) vessel.

It is very important to know what navigation lights are telling you. Is this vessel coming toward you or going away? Is it crossing to the right (of the page) or to the left? (We cannot see a sternlight, so the vessel is probably approaching. Comparing the location of the lower light on the foremast to the higher light on the aftermast, we can conclude—even without seeing the colors of the sidelights—that the vessel is moving toward our right.)

Your green starboard light tells oncomers on your starboard side to continue on their course. You recognize that they have the right of way and you are the "give-way" vessel.

The white sternlight says "watch out for me." (Detailed explanations are provided in the following sections.)

If these three lights have been properly installed, their angles of illumination will allow you to see only one light at a time. The exception is if you see a vessel from dead ahead, when both the green and red lights are visible. (Sometimes this looks like one white light if the vessel is far away.) By the book, each separate port and starboard light is visible from dead ahead through 112½ degrees. That is, from dead ahead to two points, or 22½ degrees, abaft (behind) the beam. The sternlight is visible over a horizontal arc of 135 degrees. Since 360 degrees defines a circle (112½ degrees plus 112½ degrees plus 135 degrees equals 360 degrees), you should not be able to see more than one of these three lights at the same time except, as we've noted, when you're dead ahead of another vessel.

The masthead or steaming light is a white light. It sits in the middle of the mast on a sailboat, or on a lower mast on a powerboat. It indicates that the vessel is under power and is under way. If the vessel is more than 50 meters in length, it must have a second steaming light on an after or rear mast, with its light positioned higher than the one on the foremast. (This helps to identify the heading of the vessel when only its lights can be seen.)

If a sailboat's engine is running only to charge the batteries, the steaming light doesn't have to be lit. But if the sailboat's engine is connected to the drivetrain (in gear), even if the sails are up, the vessel is considered to be under power and the steaming light has to be on.

The lower masthead light on the foremast and the higher masthead light on the aftermast of this power vessel would indicate that it is going from our port to our starboard even if we couldn't see its green starboard side light.

The anchor light is a white light on top of a mast or post that can be seen from all around. It signals that the vessel is at anchor. Since the vessel is not under way, the running lights must not be on at the same time as the anchor light. If a vessel is in a specified anchorage or well-defined mooring area, it need not have its anchor light on. Along the Eastern seaboard, for example, moorings are more typical than docks, and it would be impractical for vessels to leave their anchor lights on all the time.

Fishing boat lights: Fishing boats display a red or green light over a white light on the same mast according to the kind of fishing they're engaged in. (The reminder phrase is, "Red over white, fishing tonight.")

"Not under command" lights: A vessel showing one red light above another on the same mast is signaling that it is unable to maneuver. It may have engine trouble, or be in some other difficulty. (The morbid reminder phrase here is, "Red over red, captain is dead.")

"Restricted in ability to maneuver" lights: A vessel showing a red light over a white light over a red light on the same mast is signaling that it isn't free to maneuver wherever it wishes because of the nature of its work. (I teach my classes, "Red, white, red, full of lead.")

Pilot boat lights: Pilot boats show a white light over a red light on the same mast. Pilot boats have these lights turned on whether or not they are under way. It is common for them to be either anchored or drifting while working.

Tugboat towing lights (total length of tug and tow less than 200 meters): A power-driven vessel with a tow, having a combined length of less than 200 meters, shows a white light over a white light on the same mast and a yellow "towing light" (not a sternlight) in a vertical line above her sternlight. The vessel or barge under tow shows sidelights and an ordinary sternlight.

If, rather than a tow, the tug and its tow are traveling as a rigid "composite unit"—cabled together, for instance, with the tug pushing—only the tug will have a sternlight. The barge or ship portion ahead will have port and starboard lights.

Tugboat towing lights for a tug and tow with a total length of more than 200 meters: A tugboat with tow, having a combined length of more than 200 meters, shows a white light over a white light over a white light on the same mast as well as the previously mentioned yellow sternlight. The boat or barge being towed shows a red, green, and stern light (white).

Sailboat lights: A sailboat less than 12 meters (37 feet) long can have

- The standard red to port and green to starboard configuration; or

- An all-around (can be seen from 360 degrees) red light over an all-around green light at the masthead, regular port and starboard sidelights, plus a regular sternlight; or

- A masthead tricolor light unit showing 112½ degrees green to starboard, 112½ degrees red to port, and 135 degrees white astern. When this kind of combination light is used, the regular port and starboard lights must be turned off, along with the sternlight. This option can also have an anchor light housed in its upper portion, and a built-in strobe light. Regardless of which system is used, only one complete set of running lights can be on at a time.

Small-vessel lights: Vessels less than 7 meters (23 feet) long whose speed does not exceed 7 knots should show an all-around white light. Power vessels under 7 meters whose speed exceeds 7 knots must have the full set of navigation lights. Sailing vessels under 7 meters are not required to show an all-around white light. They need only have a white flashlight or lantern ready to show if another vessel approaches.

Here are definitions of some basic terms to help you with this section:

*Making way:* Moving through water.

*Not under command:* A vessel unable to be properly steered or maneuvered due to loss of power, loss of propeller, or some other reason. A vessel not under command may be under way and may make way through the water and is therefore unable to keep out of the way of another vessel.

*Power-driven vessel:* Any vessel (including a sailboat with its sails up) that is being propelled by machinery.

*Restricted in her ability to maneuver:* A vessel unable to move out of the way of another vessel; for example, one working on buoys or recovering other vessels or aircraft.

*Under way:* Not tied to a dock, or anchored, or aground. Note that a vessel under way does not necessarily have to be under sail or engine power. Note, too, that she does not have to be moving through the water.

## Tip 8.2  Know what oncoming lights tell you

You should understand navigation lights well enough to tell at a glance what kind of vessel is showing them, and whether "seeing the light" means you should change your course. To verify your understanding of Tip 8.1, here is a rundown on some lights, and possible combinations of lights, that you're likely to encounter on the water at night—and what they mean.

**Red only.**  This is the port forward part of a sailboat that is traveling from your right to your left. It could also be a powerboat with its steaming light off or not working. This vessel has the right of way and is the "stand-on" vessel. Red means you stop or alter course to pass behind.

**Red with white above.**  This is the port forward part of a vessel under power (either a sailboat or powerboat) traveling from your right to your left. This vessel is the stand-on vessel. Red means you must stop or alter course to pass behind it.

**Red with two whites above.**  This is the port forward part of a vessel longer than 50 meters, under power. This is the stand-on vessel. Red means you stop or alter course. If the two whites are on the same mast, the vessel is a tugboat and it could have a tow behind. If the two white lights are on separate masts, the vessel is longer than 50 meters and you should be able to tell its bearing, based on the relative position of the one red light and two white masthead lights.

**Green only.**  This is the starboard forward part of a sailboat traveling from your left to your right. It could also be a powerboat with its steaming light off or not operating. You are the stand-on vessel, but be careful: the other vessel may not know that, or may not see you.

**Green with white above.**  This is the starboard forward part of a vessel under power (either a sailboat or powerboat) traveling from your left to your right. You are the stand-on vessel. Again, be careful: the other vessel may not know that, or may not see you.

**Green with two whites above.** This is the starboard forward part of a vessel longer than 50 meters, under power. You are the stand-on vessel, but be careful: the other vessel may not know that, or may not see you. If the two whites are on the same mast, the vessel is a tugboat and it could have a tow behind. If the two white lights are on separate masts, the vessel is longer than 50 meters and you should be able to tell its bearing, based on the relative position of the one green light and two white masthead lights.

**One white light at water level.** This can be one of four things:

1. The sternlight of a vessel clear ahead.

2. A combination of green and red bow lights set close together, appearing as white, on a vessel heading directly at you.

3. The running light of a powerboat under 7 meters whose speed does not exceed 7 knots.

4. The sole navigation light of a sailboat under 7 meters in length, or a vessel under oars.

**One all-around white light high above water level.** This is a vessel at anchor.

**Red and green lights.** This is the bow of a sailboat heading directly toward you. If you can see both the red and green lights clearly, take action fast.

**Red and green lights with one white light above.** This is the bow of a vessel under power (either a sailboat or a powerboat) heading directly toward you. Time for quick action.

**Red and green lights with two white lights above.** This is the bow of a power vessel longer than 50 meters heading directly toward you. Get out of the way. Because of the length of the boat, the two white lights are set some distance apart (one near the bow and the other near the stern). The light toward the stern is higher than the forward light. In this way, you can gauge the track of the vessel by the relative position of the two lights. If the higher light is on the right, the vessel is moving from your right to your left. If the higher light is on the left, the vessel will pass to your right. If the two lights are aligned, one above the other, you are directly in the path of the approaching vessel.

**Red over white (on the same mast, along with any other deck-level navigation light).** This is a fishing boat at work. ("Red over white, fishing tonight.") Keep clear, there may be nets or lines out.

**Green over white (on the same mast, along with any other deck-level navigation light).** This is a fishing boat engaged in trawling (fishing while under way). Careful—it may have long lines following it.

**Red over red (on the same mast, along with any other deck-level navigation light).** This vessel is not under command. It is not anchored and it is under way. ("Red over red, captain is dead.") Steer clear.

**White over red (on the same mast, along with any other deck-level navigation light).** This is a pilot boat under way.

**All white deck lights illuminated.** This is any vessel at anchor. Vessels of 100 meters or more must illuminate their decks.

**White over white (same mast, along with any other deck-level navigation light).** This is a tugboat engaged in towing, the entire length of the tug and its tow being less than 200 meters. The barge or vessel being towed will have the necessary navigation lights. The tug may be towing alongside (at which point the tug and its tow will have sternlights), or it may be pushing ahead.

Recognition becomes even more important at dusk when reflections and shadows make it difficult to discern shapes and directions. Here we see this vessel's sternlight. A clear understanding
of navigation lights is essential for safe boating at night.

**White over white over white (same mast, along with any other deck-level navigation light).** This is a tugboat engaged in towing, the entire length of the tug and its tow being greater than 200 meters. Exercise great caution here.

**Red over white over red (same mast, along with any other deck-level navigation light).** This is a vessel restricted in her ability to maneuver. Stay clear and give her plenty of sea room.

**Red, green, or white light high above the water.** This is a sailboat with its running lights at the masthead (see Tip 8.1).

Notes: If any of these red, green, or white lights are flashing slowly (under 50 times a minute), they might not be on a vessel. Land-based vehicle and traffic lights often are mistaken for vessel lights or channel markers in coastal or shoreside areas. While these mirages have been the basis of many salty tales, they have also lured many boats onto the rocks.

## Tip 8.3 Protect your night vision

After several minutes in darkness at night, the pupils of your eyes are fully dilated. Exposure to white light quickly causes them to constrict again, leaving you with poor night vision until they can readjust. This can be a hazard if you are about to dock your boat.

If you or someone else needs to use a flashlight at night, be careful where the beam is shone. Better yet, have a flashlight ready that has a red or amber lens. Light in either of those colors won't cause temporary night blindness.

If you need to use a flashlight to spot markers, moorings, or your dock at night, the flashlight should be held overboard and pointed away from the boat before it is turned on. Take care that the light isn't allowed to spill inboard, where it might reflect off fiberglass or other light surfaces. Tell your crew to extinguish the light before bringing it back on board.

As an extra measure of night safety, install amber or red lamps in some of your cabin lights. That way a suddenly opened hatch won't blind someone on deck.

## Tip 8.4 Don't shine a light at other boats

It isn't legal to operate a boat at night with a searchlight on. Searchlights may be used for short intervals to locate something, but they should never be used as "driving lights." Aside from being rude, it's dangerous to shine a bright light at another vessel. You could temporarily blind the crew (see Tip 8.3) and cause an accident—very likely involving you.

If you need to use a light to call attention to your boat, then shine the light on your hull, cabintop, or deck. If you are in a sailboat, shine the light on the sails. That makes a big, white signal that everyone can see without being blinded.

## Chapter 9

# HEAVY WEATHER

My log reads: "1645, July 12th, approx. 1.5 miles southwest of Virgin Gorda's Mountain Point. Heading to round Mosquito Island and into the Sound to find anchorage for the night. Interesting experience…. Twenty minutes ago sky was generally clear, high spotty clouds. Winds at about 18 to 20 knots (no wind-speed indicator on this one) and steady. Beautiful balmy day. We were close-hauled toward the island making 7 knots. Mattee spotted black cloud on the horizon east-northeast of our location, almost dark enough to be big fire. At first, it was too far for concern, but it grew quickly, approaching us like an on-rushing locomotive. In less than 10 minutes, maybe 15, it was dead ahead and huge. Windspeed quickly spiked, water got nasty. Furled the headsail, no time to drop the main. Mattee and I only experienced sailors aboard, other crew too inexperienced to have them go forward. Snugged up mainsheet all the way, got engine running, and headed directly into this ominous black wall trying to find the eye of the damn wind. Howling was fierce, bow punching through waves, stripping off the top 12 inches of water, which came across the cabintop like a thick blanket and (without permission) dumped itself into the cockpit. Thank goodness the water was warm. I had crew sit tight in the cockpit, they thought it was funny, better to have them laugh than to be scared. Stayed slightly off the wind to keep the main from flogging and ripping itself to shreds. Saw Seal Dogs Island off to my port before it hit, so knew I had lots of open water if I could hold the course. Pleased that this (chartered) Beneteau 550 handled so well and afforded me the power to punch through it. One forward-facing port on the deck was open, scooping in water by the buckets. Our bunk got soaked. Liz and Charlie's bunk dry. Didn't check Bernie and Corie's. Water spray blasting back at me really stung and was like freezing needles—what contrast. It seemed like eternity, but after about 15 minutes it was gone as fast as it came. Kept asking myself 'When should I tell them to put life vests on?' It's clear now, the black devil disappearing behind us. They're still up there laughing. I hope I can read this later—I'm shaking like a leaf. Wonder how Stu did?"

## Tip 9.1 Secure all hatches and ports

Once you realize that seas are building or that the weather is deteriorating, take immediate action. Close all hatches and ports. Don't make this a leisurely exercise: Act as though your life and the lives of your passengers depend on it. They might. You should also close the companionway hatch boards.

If you're planning a long cruise that includes any likelihood of heavy weather or high seas (such as coastal cruising), devise a means to secure your companionway hatch boards and slide from inside the vessel, to be sure they do not inadvertently open. You might have to ride out a bad storm below decks, and coping with that isn't something you should leave to spur-of-the-moment ingenuity.

The key to safe boating in heavy weather is to keep warm and dry. Thermal underwear, full boots, and good foul-weather gear can make the difference between comfort and seasickness.

## Tip 9.2  Have all hands wear life preservers

There is nothing sissified about wearing life preservers, so wear them. They provide the same kind of insurance that seat belts provide. You never know when something may happen to propel one of your passengers or crew into the drink, and in heavy weather the potential for that occurrence goes up dramatically.

If you refuse to wear life preservers—as we did—because you are in calm, balmy weather, as soon as you realize that conditions are worsening, make sure everyone is wearing life preservers. For crew working on deck, mandatory safety gear should also include a harness and tether (see Tip 9.4).

## Tip 9.3  Sound the alarm

When conditions worsen, send a warning to other boaters by transmitting a Securite message over the VHF. If you feel you are in jeopardy, contact the Coast Guard or send a Pan-Pan message to alert other boaters of your situation.

Most importantly, take the time now to review Tip 4.8 for the proper way to transmit these warning messages.

## Tip 9.4  Let no one go forward without a tether

Before you set out and before conditions get rough, rig a jack line, a strong line running down the center of the boat from bow to stern and fastened to sturdy, through-bolted fittings. (If you do any serious cruising, your vessel should have a permanently rigged jack line.)

This line should be as far inboard as possible. If you aren't able to rig a single line running amidships, then rig one jack line on the port side and one on the starboard side, each running from the stern quarter to the bow. Whenever crewmembers have to work up forward, insist that they wear a harness with a tether, and always have the tether clipped to the jack line.

Never clip a tether to one of the lifelines. "Lifelines" is a misnomer; they would be better named "litelines." First, lifelines usually aren't strong enough to take the sudden shock of someone weighing more than 100 pounds falling overboard. Second, they run too close to the edge of the boat. If a crewmember falls overboard with a 5-foot or 6-foot tether secured to a lifeline, there is a real risk of his or her being dragged alongside under water.

## Tip 9.5  Reduce sail well in advance of a weather threat

As soon as there is the slightest chance of foul weather, reduce your sail area. Reef your sails as required. Your mainsail should either be lowered and well lashed to the boom, or reefed to the lowest point appropriate for prevailing conditions. In winds up to 40 knots, it can be better to have a storm jib or a reefed (or furled) headsail, rather than no sail at all, because this acts like an airplane's vertical stabilizer to counteract any yawing motion. In severe gales and storms, the sails should be lowered and lashed in place.

Whether the conditions are rough or not, a harness is always a good idea when working on a rocking deck. Keep the tether secured inboard (a harness attached to the lifelines will let you fall overboard and drag you through the water).

Harnesses like this one may also be built into a life vest or a foul-weather jacket.

The log in the introduction to this chapter is an accurate account of a nasty situation, and we were lucky. Had the storm worsened, it would have been tricky and dangerous to reduce the mainsail area. Lesson learned: The decision to reduce sail should have come at the first hint of trouble. Although I feel we acted quickly, our lightly experienced crew had just enough time to furl the headsail and close all but one of the hatches before we plunged headlong into the gale and cresting waves. Had we not acted when we did, and had all the hatches been left open, the outcome might have been worse— probably not disastrous, but certainly a call for the bucket brigade. I monitored the weather channel in the mornings and evenings and there was no report of impending squalls. And, I was paying attention to the VHF, but word of the deteriorating weather came across the air only well after we began to reduce sail. You can never act quickly enough.

## Tip 9.6  Prepare ahead of time to be dry

Unless you have sophisticated weather-monitoring equipment on board, you have no way of knowing in advance how long you may have to endure a bout of heavy weather. Your ability to work effectively could be seriously hampered if you get chilled and wet; so besides reducing sail, closing windows or ports, or stowing gear, prepare yourself and your crewmembers to stay warm and dry. Put on foul-weather gear early. If you have deck boots, wear them (warm feet make a big difference). Keep your head warm, and if you have waterproof gloves, wear those, too. The more comfortable you are, the longer you will be able to work in adverse conditions.

## Tip 9.7  Stay calm

The odds favor you and your boat making it through the roughest conditions, as long as you take all precautions (wear harnesses, close hatches and ports, reduce sail early, and so on). The most important key to safety in heavy weather is to remain calm. Keep your crew calm. Give orderly instructions in a relaxed manner. No matter how big the butterflies in your stomach may be, your crew will help you through if you maintain their confidence in your ability as a skipper.

Unless the most serious crisis occurs (that is, the vessel is actually sinking), stay with the boat. Making an irrational decision to abandon ship just because things are rough is not an example of staying calm. Your greatest chance of survival comes with the calm, controlled management of everything that is going on, difficult as that may be at the time. If you are planning a major coastal trip where you might face severe conditions, talk through your emergency plans with your crew ahead of time. Rehearse the "what-ifs," consider the worst-case scenarios, and don't wait until something serious happens to figure out how you and your crew will handle it.

## Tip 9.8  You bear the burden

Some things aren't easy to hear; but it's better that you hear this from me now than from yourself later in a bad situation: If you get into trouble out there, it will most likely be because you screwed up. If your engine quits because it ran out of oil, no one will offer any sympathy when you say, "Hey, I didn't know this thing had a dipstick." If your flashlight doesn't work or your flare gun is rusted solid, guess what? You screwed up. Plan ahead.

The responsibility is the same whether you are going on a one-hour joyride in the bay or a one-year excursion to Mexico. Just because your ride will be short, it doesn't mean you should be less prepared. When you go on the water, be prepared. If you aren't, don't go. It's that simple.

## Tip 9.9  Lash before you leave

When preparing for an ocean trip, secure everything that is below decks. Make sure that cabinet doors will stay shut, put shock cords in front of your books, stow all sea bags, and remove loose items from settees or countertops. All objects should be secured so that they cannot move sideways or up—a vessel in nasty water doesn't always know up from down. In heavy seas, loose items get easily tossed around and threaten the safety of anyone in the cabin. In the midst of a serious pounding, a cabin that stays shipshape will help keep nerves from frazzling and will assist you and your crew in executing below deck chores.

## Tip 9.10  Tune in

Most VHF radios have weather channels. In areas of inclement weather, especially in stormy seasons, listen to the forecasts every two hours.

Search the horizon for dark spots. As you read in the introduction to this chapter, surprises can happen.

Pay attention to the chatter on your VHF. In addition to regular marine safety information, you may learn of radical changes in the weather.

## Tip 9.11 Where to find a safe haven

The usual advice is to stay clear of harbors and shorelines during a storm. It is very tricky to seek the safety of a harbor by entering its channel in steep seas, extreme winds, and reduced visibility. If you are at sea and the weather is nasty, the best advice is to ride it out at sea. You may get sick but you'll be safe.

Most importantly, call the Coast Guard and notify them of your position and your situation.

Meanwhile, study these "ifs:"

If the situation gets miserable and you are in open water, stay with your boat unless you are absolutely certain that it is going down. Lash or secure the wheel or tiller to one side, go below, secure everything, and hang on. On powerboats, get off the flybridge.

If you are in a bay or anchorage and the storm brings onshore winds (known as a "lee shore"—the winds are blowing from the water to the shore), you need to monitor your position and your anchor's bite on a minute-by-minute basis.

If you have loran or GPS, use them to monitor your position.

If your anchor begins to drag toward shore, switch your engine on, put it in gear, and take some of the load off the anchor and its rode. If you can safely get a second anchor out, either by motoring forward, dropping the second anchor and slowly slipping back, or by going out in your dinghy and dropping the second anchor, do so. If you cannot get a second anchor forward of your boat, drop the anchor right off the side and pay out plenty of line. With any luck, it will dig in when its time comes. Absolutely do not attempt a dinghy drop in hazardous seas or dangerous conditions.

If the situation worsens and your anchor is dragging faster than you can control the boat, you have only two decisions to make. If you can safely get ashore, do so immediately. If not, move the boat farther from shore.

If the winds are blowing off the shore (called a "weather shore" wind) the chance of your boat ending on the beach or rocks is slim. However, the chances of the anchor's dragging are about the same. Again, monitor your position, set a second anchor if you can, and if conditions worsen, attempt to get ashore.

If you choose to venture into a storm from a partially protected anchorage, you're on your own, and you will have only instinct and adrenaline to guide you.

## Chapter 10

# MISCELLANY

When you pull everything out of your ditty bag, I promise there will be some loose odds and ends in the bottom. And so it is with this chapter.

### Tip 10.1  Boating in the digital era

Digital technology has brought many wonderful benefits to boating. Consider, for example, the power of a handheld GPS receiver, the efficiency of a portable VHF radio, and the charting capabilities of onboard computers and Weatherfax printers. While on land, or via a cellular modem, a great resource can be found in another offshoot of the digital revolution: the World Wide Web.

The Web contains a treasure chest of marine information. Here's a starter list of hot Web sites that you can investigate and supplement.

| FACILITY | URL (PRECEDED BY http://www.) |
|---|---|
| *Boat/US* home page | boatus.com |
| *Cruising World* and *Sailing World* magazines | sailingworld.com |
| Earth view | fourmilab.ch/earthview/vplanet.html |
| Federal Communications Commission (FCC) | fcc.gov/wtb/avinarsrv.html |
| GPS and links to other related pages | rentecusa.com/gpssites.html |
| Hydromechanics Directorate | 50.tg.navy.mil |
| IYRU home page | sailing.org/ |
| Knots on the web | earlham.edu/suber/knotlink/html |
| National Oceanic and | |
|     Atmospheric Administration (NOAA) | ogp.noaa.gov.enso |
| National Weather Service | (NWS)NWS.MBAY |
| Nautical links to the net | gpu.srv.ualberta.cal~sjones/index.html |
| And more good links . . . | gosailing.com/ |
| *48° North* magazine | 48north.com/ |
| PHRF numbers for North California | |
|     and New England | well.com/user/pk/YRAphrf.html |
| Real-time SF Bay wind patterns | sfbay7.wr.usgs.gov.wind |
| Singlehanded Sailing Society | sfbaysss.org/ |
| Tall ships and maritime museums | community.bellcore.com/mbr/ |
| |     sailing-page.html |
| Tide Predictions, USA Coast | opsd.nos.noaa.gov/tideframe.htm |
| U.S. Coast Guard Local Notices to Mariners | navcen.uscg.mil/lnm/lnm.htm |
| U.S. Coast Guard nav info | navcen.uscg.mil/gps/ggcnininfo/ |
| |     IOC-CAR.TXT |
| Waypoint 1 | e-media.co.nz/wp1/default.htm |
| Weather | weather.com/twc/homepage.twc |
| West Marine home page | westmarine.com |
| WoodenBoat magazine | hypernet.com/WoodenBoat/ |
| |     WoodenBoat.html |

## Tip 10.2  The FCC Telecommunications Act of 1996

The Telecommunications Act of 1996 went into effect on February 8, 1996. It contains numerous changes to previous rulings, including new criteria for obtaining a license and a modification to the fee structures. Here are the highlights:

As far as VHF licenses are concerned, there are two categories of vessels.

*Compulsory ships* include large passenger or cargo ships that travel on the open sea, and passenger ships that travel along the coast.

Compulsory ships are required by the Telecommunications Act (and by international agreements) to be equipped with a radio station (and the associated license) for long-distance or coastal radio communications.

*Voluntary ships* are smaller vessels used for recreation (sailing, diving, fishing, water-skiing, and such).

Voluntary ships are not required to carry radio stations but may be so equipped by choice.

**What you can use**: The following marine radio equipment may be used aboard a ship. If the ship must be licensed (according to its category), all equipment is authorized under a single ship-radio-station license.

- VHF radiotelephone, 156 to 162 MHz, used for voice communications with other ships and coast stations over short distances.

- Radar, used for navigating, direction-finding, locating positions, and ship-traffic control.

- EPIRB (Emergency Position-Indicating Radio Beacon), used when a ship is in distress, to transmit a radio signal marking the ship's location. (Extreme care must be taken to prevent inadvertent activation, and batteries should be replaced prior to expiration date.)

- Single-sideband radiotelephone, 2 to 27.5 MHz, used to communicate over medium and long distances (hundreds to thousands of nautical miles).

- Satellite radio, used to communicate by means of voice, data, or by direct printing, via satellites.

- Radiotelegraph, used to communicate by means of Morse code, facsimile, or narrow-band direct-printing.

- Survival craft radio, used for survival purposes only from lifeboats and rafts.

- Onboard radio: low-powered radios used for onboard communications or for authorized short-range communications directly associated with ship operations.

- GPS, loran, and depth finders, used for navigation and position-finding. No license is required for these.

- Citizens band (CB) radio, used for low-powered short-range communication. A citizens band license is required from the FCC (see address on page 208).

### Who needs a license?

*Voluntary ships.* As long as your vessel does not meet the criteria for compulsory ships (below), you do not need a license to operate a marine VHF radio, radar, or EPIRB while operating in United States domestic waters. Although a license is no longer required, you may still obtain a license and call sign from the FCC (see *How to Contact the FCC* at the end of this section). Note: Be sure to check "tow boats" in the next section.

*Compulsory ships.* Vessels that *do* require a license are:

- Cargo ships over 300 gross tons navigating in the open sea.

- Ships certified by the U.S. Coast Guard to carry more than six passengers for hire in the open sea or tidewaters of the U.S.

- Power-driven ships over 20 meters (60 feet) in length on navigable waterways.

- Ships of more than 100 gross tons certified by the U.S. Coast Guard to carry at least one passenger on navigable waterways.

- Tow boats of more than 7.8 meters (24 feet) in length on navigable waterways.

- Uninspected commercial fishing–industry vessels that are required to carry a VHF radio.

**What does "domestic" mean?** This class includes ships that do not travel to foreign ports or transmit radio communications to foreign stations. (Note: Possession of a VHF is legal on international waters without a radio license as long as neither of the conditions in the previous sentence is violated.)

**No license for voluntary ships.** For voluntary ships, a license is not required (but you may obtain one) for marine VHF radios, EPIRBs (any class), radar, GPS, loran, charters, plotters, fish finders, or depth finders. CB radios require an FCC citizens band license. Ships that use single-sideband radios, satellite communications, or telegraphy must be licensed by the FCC.

American boaters who qualify as voluntary ships and cross into Canada or Mexico do need a ship-station license and an operator's permit for marine VHF radios.

**How much is a license if I want one?** As of February 8, 1996, there is no longer a "regulatory fee," but there is still a "filing fee." However, this has changed in the past and very well could change again. Be sure to check FCC Form 506 for any applicable fees and include them, if required, when you mail the form.

**Is a license needed for Digital Selective Calling (DSC)?** You must obtain a nine-digit maritime mobile service identity (MMSI) and have it programmed into the unit before you can legally transmit. (To obtain an MMSI, you need to file FCC Form 506. For current information on how to apply for this license, contact the FCC at 800-322-1117.) (See Tip 10.3, Digital Selective Calling.)

**Do I need to renew my existing license?** If you own a voluntary ship using the aforementioned equipment, you do not need to renew your license. However, you may still renew your license and retain your call sign by filing a renewal with the FCC.

**Do I need a radiotelephone operator's permit?** If you plan to dock in a foreign port, or if you communicate with foreign coast or ship stations, you *must* have a Restricted Radiotelephone Operator Permit. However, if you plan to sail only in domestic or international waters without docking in any foreign ports and without communicating with foreign coast stations, *and* your radio operates only on VHF frequencies, you do not need an operator permit.

What is the difference between a ship-radio-station license and a restricted radiotelephone operator permit? The ship-radio-station license authorizes the *radio equipment* aboard a ship. The restricted radiotelephone operator permit authorizes a specific *person* to communicate with foreign stations or use certain radio equipment.

How do I get a ship-radio-station license? Obtain FCC Form 506 from a local chandler or from the FCC (see *How do I contact the FCC?* below).

How do I get a restricted radiotelephone operator permit? Obtain FCC Form 753 from the FCC (see address in *How do I contact the FCC?* below).

May I operate a marine radio while my application is being processed? Yes. However, your application has to be in the mail (there is a 90-day temporary permit attached to the form that you keep).

What do I do with my license if my vessel is sold? Send your ship-station license marked "CANCEL" back to the FCC (see address in *How do I contact the FCC?* below).

May I use my handheld marine VHF radio on land? Not without a special marine-utility-station license. You need FCC Form 503 to apply (see address below).

How do I contact the FCC? Write to Federal Communications Commission (FCC), 1270 Fairfield Road, Gettysburg, PA 17325-7245, or call: 800-418-3676 for forms, or 800-322-1117 for consumer assistance. Browse the FCC Web site: http://www.fcc.gov.wtb.avmarsrv.html.

## Tip 10.3  Digital Selective Calling (DSC)

DSC radios automatically maintain a watch on marine VHF Channel 70, which will be used as an automatic DSC hailing channel. For it to operate properly, you need a maritime mobile service identity (MMSI) number programmed into your radio. It acts as a "phone number" for your radio. With it, you can call other DSC radios or coast stations directly using their MMSI and you can communicate with commercial vessels that are required to carry DSC radios, beginning February 1, 1999.

Beginning June 17, 1999, marine radio manufacturers must include a DSC capability in new radios. (Recreational boaters are not required to buy a DSC radio, but may do so at their option.)

# INDEX

# INDEX